Revelation

Christianity and Judaism — The Formative Categories

Revelation

The Torah and The Bible

Jacob Neusner
Bruce D. Chilton

TRINITY PRESS INTERNATIONAL
Valley Forge, Pennsylvania

Trinity Press International, P.O. Box 851, Valley Forge, PA 19482–0851

Library of Congress Cataloging-in-Publication Data

Neusner, Jacob, 1932–
    Revelation : the Torah and the Bible / Jacob Neusner, Bruce D.
Chilton.
        p.   cm. – (Christianity and Judaism, the formative
categories)
    Includes bibliographical references and index.
    ISBN 1-56338-124-9 (pbk. : alk. paper)
    1. Revelation (Jewish theology) 2. Revelation. 3. Judaism–
Doctrines. 4. Theology, Doctrinal.   I. Chilton, Bruce.
II. Title.   III. Series: Neusner, Jacob, 1932–   Christianity and
Judaism, the formative categories.
BM645.R5N48   1995
220–dc20   95-37159
                                                                           CIP

Printed in the United States of America

95   96   97   98   99   10   9   8   7   6   5   4   3   2   1

Contents

Preface

Christianity and Judaism, along with Islam, by their own word seek to reach the same God, but each takes its own path. All three invoke the same authority, Abraham and Sarah, represented by the same Scripture, and all three worship the one and only God. At the same time, each distinguishes itself from the other two, finding important differences at specific points and maintaining that it, and not the others, accurately records what that one, unique God has said. Sustained argument takes place when people who agree on premises and principles also disagree on propositions and conclusions, and therefore Judaism, Islam, and Christianity can sustain — and for determinate periods in the past have indeed mounted — cogent and illuminating arguments against one another.

Among the three, because of the intimacy of their relationship — historical and geographical alike — Judaism and Christianity have mounted the closest dialogue, which in the very recent past has turned cordial. In the past they were uncomprehending and expressed contempt for each other's absurdities. Imputations of guilt, recriminations, not to mention exclusion and even murder, ruined the possibilities for the mutual illumination of self-respecting and mutually honored partners in dialogue. Now, for the first time in the United States and the English-speaking world in general, differences between those two complex sets of religious traditions come under discussion free of rancor and recrimination. Consequently, outlining the points of concurrence and conflict may take place in a spirit of enlightenment and friendship. There arises no need to negotiate, or even place limits upon difference, but only to understand the other more fully and more accurately.

Our purpose here is to compare and contrast the paramount theological categories of Judaism and Christianity, each meaning to inform the other of the main points of the classical theology of his religious tradition on matters of concern to the other. Moreover, each takes seriously and comments on the other's presentation of his position, pointing to likenesses and differences. So we mean to describe, then compare and contrast, the main theological structures on which our respective faiths are constructed.

We do not propose to obscure theological difference or to sidestep profound disagreement in quest of the socially useful goal of amity. To the contrary, we seek a different goal from theological negotiation; neither is "liberal" about his own beliefs, let alone "tolerant" of the choices made by the other. Each believes in his tradition and its affirmations, and each without apology or excuse practices that tradition. Neither proposes to permit long-term friendship and partnership in intellectual projects to impose conditions on the integrity of his faith, nor wants the other to. Both of us are educators and scholars, firm in the conviction that knowledge and understanding affirm our convictions but also demand respect for differing ones. We each seek to grasp the rationality of the views of the other, in full awareness that it is a different rationality.

.   The present work is one of the three volumes that together constitute the series we have entitled Christianity and Judaism — The Formative Categories. In the series, we propose to provide the faithful of both Judaism and Christianity with an informative, factual account of how, in their classical formulations, Christianity and Judaism addressed the same issues and set forth their own distinctive programs and sets of propositions. This is plausible and productive for several reasons.

First, Jews and Christians have lived side by side for nearly two thousand years; each group knows a great deal about the other. We have been neighbors for a long time, and now we are striving to become friends. While neither proposes to surrender the slightest point of distinctiveness, while both affirm the ultimate difference of the one from the other, and while both parties differ about how we know the same God and about what that God has made manifest to us — we concur that we really do worship the same God. Hence the possibility of educating ourselves about the other emerges: we disagree about the same things while also agreeing in many areas.

Second, because Christianity and Judaism in structure and even system are so much alike, it is possible to compare their theological formulations of the same questions, and the answers. Because they so vigorously disagree on the main points, it is productive and interesting to do this, though we do not mean here to carry forward the centuries-old disputations between the two great religious traditions of the West.

Third, because Christianity and Judaism (along with Islam) today confront as partners the challenges of militant secularism and proselytizing atheism, we find ourselves drawn together to address a common enemy. From the late eighteenth century to nearly our own day, practitioners of Judaism stood by while ethnic Jews allied the Jewish population with militant secularism. Nearly all Jews, including practitioners of Judaism ("Judaists"), took for granted, and with ample cause, that only in a neutral, secular society could Jews survive as a distinct group and that only in a neutral political world could Judaism be practiced. Moreover, communal secularism within Jewry held together the religious sector of the community, the Judaists, and the secular sector, the solely ethnic Jews. Only in the most recent past has a different perspective on the imperatives of the public square reshaped this vision; now a growing minority within the Jewish community finds friends outside not among militant secularists but in Christians of goodwill — Roman Catholic, Protestant, and Orthodox. With them Judaists make common cause in a number of shared projects, even while carefully agreeing to set aside all theological discourse. The Judaic partner in these books concurs with this minority view. Judaists and Christians, loyal to their respective faiths, recognize urgent, shared commitments to the social order.

Now this very new, but very promising, recognition of mutuality of interest calls for precisely the kinds of books that we — the two authors of these volumes — mean to write together. For mutuality of interest depends in the end upon mutuality of understanding. By this we mean that we simply have to get to know one another better than we now do. The shared labors for the public interest are best carried out by people who, agreeing to disagree on some things and to work together on others, deeply respect and fully understand the difference that separates them. And this requires knowledge, not the pretense that some subjects lie beyond all discourse. Precisely what the body of Christ means to the Christian, or the election of Israel (the holy people) to the Judaist, what the Torah tells the Judaist and the Bible the Christian, how God is made manifest in this world, that is, is "incarnate," to both Judaist and Christian — these fundamental points of commonality in structure, conflict, and system require exposition, and we promise this exposition in these books.

Ours is not a relationship of sentimentality or careful avoidance of difference. We do not believe that, at the foundations, we really are the same thing, and neither wants to become like the other or to give up any part of what makes him different from the other in the most profound layers of conviction and calling. The one writer is called to the study of the Torah as his way of life and purpose of being; the other is called to realize his identity as a child of God in the manner of Jesus. But for the one, the study of the Torah, and for the other, the imitation of Christ carry learning beyond the boundaries of the Torah or of Church, respectively. Each finds his work possible only through learning more about the religion of the other. And both maintain that sound learning and authentic understanding of their respective faiths demand attention to the near-at-hand religion of the other.

Still, we work together in a personal, not a theological, partnership. The two authors are longtime friends, and we come in an irenic spirit, genuinely fond of each other and also respectful of the call that each acknowledges God has vouchsafed to the other. We cannot explain how God has spoken in such different terms to so many people. We do not know why God has made us so different from each other — all the while seeking to serve that one and the same true God. But we know that within the traditions that shape our lives and minds we are constrained to recognize that the other is possessed of the same revelation that we revere. Since the Judaic partner understands that Christianity's "Old Testament" is his "written Torah," and since the

Christian partner recognizes the same fact, both share the common ground that here God has said the same thing to each, and on that account comparison and contrast form options that we now wish to explore.

Firm in our convictions, neither of us asks the other to surrender his beliefs; we are not going to say which of us, from God's viewpoint, is right. In the fullness of time God will not only decide but make the decision known. For the interim we accept the situation of indeterminacy: each of us is sure he is right, but neither finds the other's assent — therefore, conversion — a condition of mutual education. There is a very practical reason for this shared decision, even while for the two of us it also represents a dimension of religious conviction to leave for God the final choice.

If we do not choose here to debate who is right, it is in some part because that debate has gone on through long centuries, and we doubt much is left to be said. Nor has the debate proved illuminating or productive, when framed in terms of truth and error. But we do wish to provide for faithful believers in Judaism and Christianity a systematic and fair-minded picture of what both religions say about the same things. The differences coincide: Torah or Bible (volume 1), Israel or Church (volume 2), the media of God's this-worldly incarnation (volume 3). In our view religious dialogue, including debate, benefits us all. Our theory — and here we speak only for ourselves personally, and not for the Church or the Torah — is that each has learned something about God that the other must want to know, even while each of us knows full well that the criterion of truth rests, as it has always rested, for Judaism with the Torah, and for Christianity with Christ. But that candid affirmation of difference defines not the end but only the beginning of the dialogue that we believe finally serves the greater glory of the one God.

Both value "the Book," meaning, the Hebrew Scriptures of ancient Israel. What our regard for the Scriptures means should be made clear, since the issues that divide us are theological and not exegetical. Many hold that because Judaism and Christianity share the same Scriptures — the written Torah and the Old Testament being identical for the most part — the debate between them concerns the meaning of those writings. We take a different view. Our commonalities and differences do not involve only how we read the received and revealed Scriptures but what we know about God, which to be sure is related to those Scriptures. Knowledge of God comes from theology, not from literary criticism or the exegesis of sources.

Therefore, we frame our comparisons in theological terms: God, the body of faith, the presence of God in the world, rather than in the contrasts between one party's reading of pertinent verses of Scripture and the other party's reading of those same verses. The reason is that theology does not recapitulate Scripture; but the exegesis of Scripture does recapitulate theology. The further reason is that for neither party is the Scripture of ancient Israel the sole and complete account of God's revelation to humanity. Christianity requires the New Testament, Judaism, the oral part of the Torah; so the issue is not exegetical at all. The question is how we fill with meaning the shared and common generative categories of the theological structure on which both build their systems: God, Torah, Israel for Judaism; God, Christ, Church for Christianity.

We underline, therefore, that for each of us, Israelite Scripture, though held in common, is contingent, because each of us complements the shared Scriptures with further revelation. Judaism knows these Scriptures as the written part, which, along with the oral part, comprises the one whole Torah that God gave ("revealed") to Moses, our Rabbi, at Mount Sinai. Christianity knows these same Scriptures as the Old Testament, which, along with the New Testament, comprises the Bible, the word of God. Because of the rich heritage of Scripture, with its ethics and morality and its account of what God wants of humanity, who God is, and what we are, many have concluded that a unitary "Judeo-Christian tradition" defines the common religion of the West; Judaism and Christianity then are supposed to differ on details but concur on the main points. The opposite is the fact, and here we propose a different reading of the relationship between the two heirs of ancient Israel in the West.

Specifically, we spell out how, because they concur on so much, the two religious traditions differ in a very explicit and precise way. They talk about the same things; they invoke the same evidence; they rest their respective cases on the same

premises of thought and rules of argument. And they profoundly differ. They divide on precisely what unites them, and
their shared agenda of faith in and love for God accounts for the
vigor and precision of their disagreements. Judaism and Christianity identify the same principal and generative categories for
the formulation of the religious life: revelation, social order, and
the encounter with God. In Judaism these categories bear the
titles "Torah," "Israel," and "God in this world," which, in the
classical documents of formative Judaism, encompasses diverse
ways in which we meet God here and now. In Christianity, the
counterparts are "the Bible," "the Church," and "Christ, the
Word of God incarnate."

In these three volumes, therefore, we identify and spell out
in an elementary way the three principal areas of communion
among, and therefore conflict between, the heirs of the same
Scripture:

1. how and what we know about God, that is, the character
   of revelation;

2. who constitutes the people to whom God is made manifest, that is, the definition of the body of the faithful; and

3. where and through whom we meet God in this world.

Each religious tradition sets forth its definition of revelation;
each defines the social order to which God has spoken, called
into being in God's service; and each knows where and how, in
this world, we meet God in human encounter.

We focus on the classical and definitive documents of the two
traditions and on their principal categories of concern. For Judaism this involves the following: the Torah, as it took shape in
the first six centuries of the Common Era, as the source of revelation; the same writings' account of who and what is "Israel";
and those documents' exposition of ways in which, in everyday
life, God enters into the situation of ordinary people: how we
meet God this morning, right here. For Christianity, the counterpart categories are the Bible (including the New Testament);
the Church as the body of Christ; and the disclosure of God's
healing and judging power by means of Christ. Those three

structuring topics are developed in the New Testament so completely that Christians embrace those texts as normative. Both authors elect to limit discussion to the classical writings, in the clear recognition that both religions unfolded through time, so that later writers expanded and recast the classical definitions and even some of the categories. We maintain that, however things changed through time, the classical formulation remains paramount.

We mean to speak to Jews and Christians who want better to understand their own religious traditions. In our view, when we identify the issues that theological teachings address, and understand the alternative positions on these issues that classical thinkers have adopted, we treat religion as vital. We cease to regard our views as self-evident and recognize that the religious decisions made by Jews and Christians represent choices made in full consideration of alternatives. Then our respective religions take on weight and consequence and become living choices among alternative truths. Only by seeing the options that have faced the framers of Judaism and Christianity in their classical writings shall we understand how, in full rationality and with entire awareness of issues and options, the founders of our respective traditions took the paths they did. When religion is reduced to platitudes and banalities, lifelessly repeating things deemed to be self-evident, it loses all consequence and forms a mere chapter in the conventions of culture. But from Judaism and Christianity, for centuries stretching backward beyond counting, faithful Israel, on the one side, and the living body of Christ, on the other, drew sustenance and found the strength to endure.

Let us not at the end lose sight of the remarkable power of these religions in times past and in our own day. The world did not make life easy for Judaism through its history in the West; and in the age of militant secularism and violently anti-Christian Communism, Christianity has found itself back in the catacombs. The century that now closes has afforded to the faith of Israel and of Christ no honor, and to the Israelite and to the Christian no respect by reason of loyalty to that vocation. Christianity outlived Communism in the Soviet Union and its colonies. At the sacrifice of home and property, even at the price of life itself, Israel resisted the world's corrosive insistence that it cease to exist and has reaffirmed its eternal calling. Whatever the choice of private persons, that social order formed by Israel, on the one side, and the Church of Jesus Christ, on the other, has endured against it all, despite it all, through all time and change. Defying fate in the certainty of faith in God's ultimate act of grace is the one thing God cannot have commanded, but it is what, in times of terrible stress, Judaic and Christian faithful have given freely and of their own volition. God can have said, and did say, "Serve me," but God could only beseech, "And trust me too."

Even God cannot coerce trust. Only Israel and the Church could give what God could ask but not compel: the gifts of the heart, love and trust, for which the loving God yearns, which only the much-loved Israel or those who have been called into the communion of the Church can yield freely, of their own volition. And that is what Israel, in response to Sinai, and the Church, in response to the empty tomb, willingly gave, and by their loyal persistence freely give today. These facts of human devotion tell us the power of the faiths that in these pages meet for a theological comparison. The stakes then are very high indeed.

The joint authors express their thanks to their respective academies, Bard College and the University of South Florida, for ongoing support for their scholarly work. At these academies, each has found ideal conditions for a life of learning, and neither takes for granted the gifts that he receives in these centers of higher learning. Both express thanks, also, to Dr. Harold Rast, Publisher of Trinity Press International, for his commitment to this project and his guidance in bringing it to fruition. If we achieve our goal of a sustained and illuminating theological encounter, it is because of his guidance and long-term commitment to our project.

BRUCE D. CHILTON
Bard College

JACOB NEUSNER
*University of South Florida
and Bard College*

Introduction

The Torah and the Bible

Both Judaism and Christianity define truth by appeal to revelation, and each religious tradition knows precisely the locus of revelation. Christianity finds the word of God in the Bible, meaning the Old Testament and the New Testament. From antiquity to our own day Judaism has identified in the Torah the same complete and exhaustive statement of God's will. Furthermore, the authoritative representation of the Torah of Sinai in a coherent statement is located in a single protean document, the Talmud of Babylonia, or Bavli. That document, created in the seventh century C.E., forms the summa of the Torah of Sinai, joining as it does the written Torah, encompassing what Christianity knows as the Old Testament, and the oral Torah, commencing with the Mishnah. So the Talmud's presentation of the entire Torah, oral and written, forms in the system of Judaism the counter to the Bible, hence, the comparison of the Bible and the Bavli.

The comparison rests on long centuries of tradition and practice. What Christianity found in Scripture and tradition, Judaism found in the Torah as set forth by the Talmud. Together with their commentaries, formed into treasures of tradition over time, the Bible, for Christianity, and the Bavli, for Judaism, have formed the court of final appeal in issues of doctrine and for Judaism normative instruction on correct deed as well. Commentaries, paraphrases, and amplifications have carried out the exegetical elaboration.

This introduction was written by Jacob Neusner and revised by Bruce D. Chilton.

Furthermore, the pattern of truth that, for the Bible and for the Bavli alike, served to state the worldview and way of life for Church and "Israel," respectively, was endowed with the status of revealed truth; the standing of tradition was granted to the ethos and ethics of the social entity.

But, while the comparison is not only justified but demanded, still, the Bavli and the Bible are quite different kinds of documents. And in the differences we see the choices people made when confronting very nearly the same problem. Specifically, when the Bible was coming into being for Christianity, the processes of tradition were doing the work that ultimately yielded the Bavli. From the second through the fourth centuries for Orthodox, Catholic Christianity, and from the second through the seventh centuries for the Judaism of the oral and written Torah, the labor of formulation and systematic statement went forward. Judaic and Christian intellectuals were sorting out the complex problems of matching their modern worlds to the words of the ancients. Both groups of intellectuals then claimed to present enduring traditions, a fundament of truth revealed of old. And, as a matter of fact, both succeeded. The Bible, which is the creation of the Orthodox, Catholic Church, and the Bavli, the gift of the sages of the academies, indeed governed Christianity and Judaism, respectively, from the time of their closure to the present day. And no other, later writing ever competed with either document for authority or standing.

But both sets of thinkers also articulated systematic and philosophical statements, which begin in first principles and rise in steady and inexorable logic to final conclusions; these are compositions of proportion, balance, cogency, and order. They are cogent systems, whole and coherent statements. They covered the principal components of the social order — the way of life, the worldview, the theory of the social entity that characterized (at least in the minds of the theologians) the life of Israel or Church. While neither religion imagined that a single book could write down that protean system and structure that God had called into being, both insisted that a single document to begin with formed the authoritative statement of the faith.

To understand the work facing the framers of the Bavli, we

have to know what writings they held to be revealed. It is not commonly understood that Judaism is not the religion of the Old Testament; it is the religion of the Torah, which encompasses an open canon, an unending process of divine revelation. The Torah, of course, begins with the Scriptures of ancient Israel, roughly comparable to the Old Testament as defined by Protestant Christianity. But the Mishnah is included in the Torah of Sinai; this is a philosophical law code produced around 200 C.E. that formed the basis for the practical government that the Judaic political authorities exercised in both the Land of Israel ("Palestine") and Babylonia; and, further, the composite of commentaries, generally in episodic form, to Scripture and the Mishnah that accumulated from the second through the fourth or fifth centuries was deemed an authoritative part of the revelation of Sinai.

Obviously, these represent diverse documents. Scripture is written in a Hebrew different from that of the Mishnah, for example; and commentaries take a form quite separate from the language of a systematic statement of law and theology, found in the Pentateuch, on the one side, and the Mishnah, on the other. Then how are they all held together and represented as a single coherent statement? That is to say, what makes these writings not only a source of valid information but a single, systematic, coherent statement, what we should call "Judaism"?

A simple question faced these heirs of the Pentateuch: How to relate the three? The Bavli's authors' answer was to write a commentary on the Mishnah and on the Scriptures alike; they understood that they would be forming a final, coherent, and cogent statement. True, the "commentary" that bore the burden of the Bavli's system would address only those passages that the authors of the Bavli found consequential. But that independent act of selectivity formed a principal intellectual labor of system building.

Christian theologians confronted a comparable problem: how to compose a diverse collection of writings into a single, coherent formation. In the case of the Christian address to the same issue, where do we look for a counterpart labor of system building through selectivity? The answer, of course, is dictated by the form of the question. We turn to the work of canonization of available writings into the Bible. There we see the theologians' work of making choices, setting forth a single statement. When we compare the systemic structures represented by the Bavli and the Bible, therefore, we can appreciate how two quite distinct groups of intellectuals worked out solutions to the same problem, and did so, as a matter of fact, in very nearly the same way, namely, by making reasoned choices. Both groups of authors set forth systems of thought, at the same time attaching to their systems the claim of tradition: God's Torah to Moses at Sinai, for Judaism; the pattern of Christian truth, for Christianity; hence the comparison of Bavli and Bible.

But then the points of difference are determined by the shared morphology, since, as a matter of obvious fact, the Bible and the Bavli are very different ways of setting forth a system. Each represents its components in a distinctive manner, the one by preserving their autonomy and calling the whole a system, the other by obscuring their originally autonomous and independent character and imparting to the whole the form of tradition. The upshot may be simply stated. The Bavli presents a system and to it, through the operative logic, imputes the standing of tradition. The Bible sets forth diverse and unsystematic traditions, received writings from many places, and to those traditions, through the act of canonization, imputes the character and structure of a system.

Let us now consider the literary media in which the two communities of intellectuals set forth their system as traditions or their traditions as system. We wish specifically to see how each has worked out its own system, what logic of discourse it has chosen, and, finally, how the system is situated in relationship to prior systematic statements.

The Bavli: Imputing Tradition to System

In the case of the Bavli, our point of entry is the identification of the odd mixture of logics utilized by the framers of the system as a whole. By "logics" we mean the ways by which statements cohere, that is, the modes of thought that explain how two or more sentences form a cogent statement. In simple language, "logic" refers here to the logic of coherent discourse. Specifically, it refers to how one sentence forms a connection to the next, so that the two make up a whole that is greater than the sum of the parts, that is, a coherent thought.

The specific issue is, What happens when two documents of quite different character meet, with one made into a commentary on the other? What forms the problem is that the Mishnah, as we shall explain, is a profoundly philosophical writing, formed into cogent units of thought, which set forth clearly argued propositions. By contrast, the Talmud of Babylonia in the aggregate is a commentary on another document (the Mishnah), and most of its completed thoughts ("paragraphs") relate to the prior document, without really relating to one another at all. So the Mishnah's appeal is to a logic of propositional discourse, while the Bavli rests upon the coherence imparted to discrete and apparently unrelated thoughts ("sentences") by a document external to itself. This problem may sound a bit abstruse, but it is the key to the representation, in writing, of a culture as traditional: everything holds together by reason of its connection to a revealed truth, handed on unimpaired from of old. And nothing new matters except that it makes sense as part of that old, revealed tradition. The one kind of discourse is argumentative and systematic; the other is episodic and occasional. The one is a statement with a beginning, middle, and end; the other, a formulation that utterly depends for order upon some prior formulation.

To grasp this problem, we have to pay attention to the character of the Bavli as a commentary on the Mishnah. The Mishnah formed a complete and coherent piece of writing, which can be read in its own terms, without reference to any other document. The Bavli, by contrast, is organized as a commentary on the Mishnah and can be grasped only in relationship to that prior writing; but the framers of the Bavli have also dismantled the Mishnah, since it is read not as a whole and coherent statement (or a set of such statements) but rather as a sequence of phrases, clauses, and free-standing sentences.

The Mishnah utilized a single logic to set forth a system that, in form as in inner structure, stood wholly autonomous and independent, a statement unto itself, with scarcely a ritual obeisance to any prior system. We can read sentences and paragraphs of the Mishnah and follow the thought, the connections between one thing and the next, with no significant difficulty (excepting the facts that are taken for granted). It is a propositional document that sets forth its ideas through standard exposition. The document followed the inexorable authority of logic, specifically, the inner logic of a topic, which dictated the order of thought and defined the contents of a particular topic. These intellectual modalities in their nature display an independence of mind, even when, in point of fact, the result of thought is a repetition of what Scripture itself has already said.

But those who received the Mishnah and handed it onward from the second century to the seventh, when the Bavli was completed, found this a considerable problem. As soon as the Mishnah made its appearance, therefore, the vast labor of explaining its meaning but especially justifying its authority was sure to get under way. The Mishnah presented one striking problem in particular. It rarely cited scriptural authority for its rules. On what basis, then, do the Mishnah's rules command Israel's obedience? This is another way of asking how the Mishnah relates to the revelation of the Torah at Sinai. Omitting scriptural proof texts bore the implicit claim to an authority independent of Scripture, an authority deriving from logic working within its own inner tensions and appealing to tests of reason and sound argument. In that striking fact the document set a new course for itself. But the question of its authorship raised problems for those who would apply its law to Israel's life.

After the formation of ancient Israelite Scripture into a holy book in Judaism, in the aftermath of the return to Zion and the creation of the Torah-book in Ezra's time (ca. 450 B.C.E.), coming generations routinely set their ideas into relationship with Scripture. They did this by citing proof texts alongside their own rules. Otherwise, in the setting of Israelite culture, the new writings could find no ready hearing. Over the six hundred years from the formation of the Torah of "Moses" in the time of Ezra, from about 450 B.C.E. to about 200 C.E., four conventional ways to accommodate new writings — new "tradition" — to the established canon of received Scripture had come to the fore.

First and simplest, a writer would sign a famous name to his book, attributing his ideas to Enoch, Adam, Jacob's sons, Jeremiah, Baruch, and any number of others, down to Ezra. But the Mishnah bore no such attribution, for example, to Moses. Implicitly, to be sure, the statement of M. Abot 1:1, "Moses received Torah from Sinai," carried the distinct notion that sayings of people on the list of authorities from Moses to nearly their own day came from God's revelation at Sinai. But no one made that premise explicit before the time of the Bavli and the Talmud of the Land of Israel. Second, an author might also imitate the style of biblical Hebrew and so try to creep into the canon by adopting the cloak of Scripture. But the Mishnah's authors ignore biblical syntax and style. Third, an author could surely claim his work was inspired by God, a new revelation for an open canon. But, as we realize, that claim makes no explicit impact on the Mishnah. Fourth, at the very least someone could link his opinions to biblical verses through their exegesis so Scripture would validate his views. The authors of the Mishnah did so only occasionally, but far more commonly stated on their own authority whatever rules they proposed to lay down.

The Hebrew of the Mishnah complicated the problem because it is totally different from the Hebrew of the Hebrew Scriptures. Its verb, for instance, makes provision for more than completed or continuing action, which is standard for the biblical Hebrew verb, but also for past and future times, subjunctive and indicative voices, and much else. The syntax is Indo-European, in that we can translate the word order of the Mishnah into any Indo-European language and come up with good sense. None of that crabbed imitation of biblical Hebrew, which makes the Dead Sea Scrolls an embarrassment to read, characterizes the Hebrew of the Mishnah. Mishnaic style is elegant, subtle, exquisite in its sensitivity to repetition, balance, pattern, and word order.

The solution to the problem of the authority of the Mishnah, that is to say, its relationship to Scripture, was worked out in the period after the closure of the Mishnah. This solution marked the beginning of the process of Mishnah commentary that culminated in the Bavli itself. The first option was to provide a myth of the origin of the contents of the Mishnah; and the second option was to link each allegation of the Mishnah, through processes of biblical (not mishnaic) exegesis, to verses of the Scriptures. These two procedures, together, would give the Mishnah the standing it needed — namely, a place in the canon of Israel, a legitimate relationship to the Torah of Moses — in order to fulfill the demands to be put to it.

So the issue was: Precisely how are these sages to present their ideas as a tradition going back to Sinai? And what will impart to these ideas coherence and cogency, so that connections between one idea and the next will yield propositions of sense and proportion? There were several ways in which the work went forward. These are represented by diverse documents that succeeded and dealt with the Mishnah. The three principal possibilities were these:

1. The Mishnah required no systematic support through exegesis of Scripture in light of mishnaic laws.

2. The Mishnah by itself provided no reliable information, and all of its propositions demanded linkage to Scripture, to which the Mishnah must be shown to be subordinate and secondary.

3. The Mishnah is an autonomous document, but closely correlated with Scripture.

The first extreme is represented by the Abot (ca. 250 C.E.), which represents the authority of the sages cited in Abot as autonomous, hence independent of Scripture. These authorities in Abot do not cite verses of Scripture, but what they say does constitute a statement of the Torah. There can be no clearer way of saying that what these authorities present in and of itself falls into the classification of the Torah. The authorship of the Tosefta (ca. 400 C.E.) takes the middle position. It very commonly cites a passage of the Mishnah and then adds to that passage an appropriate proof text. This is a quite common mode of supplementing the Mishnah.

The mediating view is taken by the Yerushalmi (the Talmud of the Land of Israel) and the Bavli (ca. 400–600 C.E.). Yerushalmi's and Bavli's authors developed a well-crafted theory of the Mishnah and its relationship to Scripture. Each rule of the Mishnah is commonly introduced, in the exegesis supplied by the two Talmuds, with the question, "What is the source of this statement?" And the answer invariably is, "As it is said," or "...written," with a verse of Scripture, that is, the written Torah, then cited. The upshot is that the source of the rules of the Mishnah (and other writings) is Scripture, not free-standing logic. The far extreme — everything in the Mishnah makes sense only as a (re)statement of Scripture or upon Scripture's authority — is taken by the Sifra, a postmishnaic compilation of exegeses on Leviticus, redacted at an indeterminate point, perhaps about 300 C.E. The Sifra systematically challenges reason (= the Mishnah), unaided by revelation (that is, exegesis of Scripture), to sustain positions taken by the Mishnah, which is cited verbatim, and everywhere proves that it cannot be done.

The final and normative solution to the problem of the authority of the Mishnah — a solution worked out in the third and fourth centuries — produced the myth of the dual Torah, oral and written, which formed the indicative and definitive trait of the Judaism that emerged from late antiquity. Tracing the unfolding of that myth leads us deep into the processes by which that Judaism took shape. The Bavli knows the theory that there is a tradition separate from, and in addition to, the written Torah. This tradition it knows as "the teachings of scribes." The Mishnah is identified as the collection of those teachings only by implication in the Bavli. We cannot point to a single passage in which explicit judgment upon the character and status of the Mishnah as a complete document is laid down. Nor is the Mishnah treated as a symbol or called "the oral Torah." But there is ample evidence, once again implicit in what happens to the Mishnah in the Bavli, to allow a reliable description of how the Bavli's founders viewed the Mishnah.

This view may be stated very simply. The Mishnah rarely cites verses of Scripture in support of its propositions. The Bavli routinely adduces scriptural bases for the Mishnah's laws. The Mishnah seldom undertakes the exegesis of verses of Scripture for any purpose. The Bavli consistently investigates the meaning of verses of Scripture and does so for a variety of purposes. Accordingly, the Bavli, subordinate as it is to the Mishnah, regards the Mishnah as subordinate to, and contingent upon, Scripture. This is why in the Bavli's view the Mishnah requires the support of proof texts of Scripture. By itself, the Mishnah exercises no autonomous authority and enjoys no independent standing or norm-setting status.

Now this brings us back, by a circuitous route, to the Bavli's explanation of its own position in relationship to the received "tradition," which is to say, to prior systemic statements in the Pentateuch and the Mishnah. The authors' solution to the problem of the standing and authority of the Mishnah dictated their answer to the question of the representation, within a received tradition, of their own system as well. It was through phrase-by-phrase commentary that the Bavli's authors justified the Mishnah as tradition and represented it as a secondary elaboration of Scripture or as invariably resting on the authority of Scripture. This form does what can be done to represent sentences of the Mishnah as related to sentences of Scripture. Moreover, this mode of writing accomplished what we may call the dismantling or deconstruction of the system of the Mishnah and the reconstruction of its bits and pieces into the system of the Bavli. The Bavli's authors never represented the Mishnah's system whole and complete and rarely acknowledged that the Mishnah consisted of more than discrete statements, to be related to some larger, cogent law that transcended the Mishnah.

Having represented the Mishnah in this way, the Bavli's authors quite naturally chose to represent their own system in the same way, that is to say, as a mere elaboration of a received tradition, a stage in the sedimentary and incremental process by which the Torah continued to come down from Sinai. And for that purpose, we hardly need to add, the mixed logics embodied in the joining of philosophical and propositional statements on the principle of fixed association to a prior text served exceedingly well. That explains how, in the Bavli, we have, in the (deceptive) form of a tradition, what is in fact an autonomous system, connected with prior systems but not continuous with them. The authors represented their own statement of an ethos, ethics, and defined social entity precisely as they did the received ones, the whole forming a single, seamless Torah revealed by God to Moses at Sinai. So much for a system to which the standing of tradition is imputed through formal means. What we have is a system in thought and cogency, portrayed as a tradition in form and style. That is one solution to the problem of cultural and religious continuity, from ancient times to this morning's revelation.

The Bible: Imputing System to Traditions

From the Judaic solution to the problem of formulating ancient Israelite traditions as a single, coherent statement, we now come to the counterpart religious world: that is, we confront Christian intellectuals also dealing with the inheritance of ancient Israel's Scriptures and facing the same problem. The parallel is exact in yet another aspect. Just as the authors of the Bavli received not only what they came to call the written Torah but also the Mishnah and other writings that had attained acceptance, hence authority, from the closure of the Mishnah to their own day, so too did the Christian intellectuals inherit more than the Old Testament. They had in hand a variety of authoritative documents to which the inspiration of the Holy Spirit was imputed. So they confronted the same problem as faced the authors of the Bavli, and it was in nearly the same terms, namely, how to sort out received documents, each of which made its own statement about a problem and followed a different solution to that problem. The Christians took a different way from the Judaic sages, producing the foundation-document of Christianity, and as a matter of fact also of Western civilization, the Bible.

What they did, specifically, was to join together the received writings as autonomous books, but to impute to the whole the standing of a cogent statement, a single and harmonious Christian truth. They did this in making the biblical canon—joining diverse traditions into a single, uniform, and (putatively) harmonious Bible, understood to be God's word. In short, the essence of the Christian solution to the problem of making a statement but also situating that statement in relationship to received tradition was to impute system to discrete traditions through a declared canon.[1] This, clearly, has similarities with the solution offered by Judaism's Bavli. That is to say, the Bavli presents a system but represents it as a tradition — from Sinai. The legitimacy of comparing the two groups of intellectuals through their ultimate statements, the Bavli and the Bible, seems to be sustained by the simple theological judgment of Henry Turner:

> The mind of the Church [in making the canon] was guided by criteria rationally devised and flexibly applied. There is no dead hand in the production of the Canon; there is rather the living action of the Holy Spirit using as He is wont the full range of the continuing life of the church to achieve His purposes in due season.[2]

We can find no better language to state, in a way interior to a system, the claim that a writing or a set of writings constitutes a system: a way of life, a worldview, an address to a particular social entity. This too is made explicit by Turner, whom we take to be a thoroughly reliable representative of Christian theology on the subject:

> There can be no doubt that the Bible is fundamentally an orthodox book, sufficient if its teaching is studied as a whole to lead to orthodox conclusions.... The Biblical data insist upon arranging themselves in certain theological patterns and cannot be forced into other moulds without violent distortion. That is the point of a famous simile of St. Irenaeus. The teaching of Scripture can be compared to a mosaic of the head of a king, but the heretics break up the pattern and reassemble it in the form of a dog or a fox.[3]

---

1. In laying matters out, we avoid entering the issues debated by Walter Bauer, *Orthodoxy and Heresy in Earliest Christianity* (Philadelphia: Fortress, 1971), translation of *Rechtgläubigkeit und Ketzerei im ältesten Christentum* (1934, supplemented by Georg Strecker, 1964). See also Henry E. W. Turner, *The Pattern of Christian Truth: A Study of the Relations between Orthodoxy and Heresy in the Early Church*, Bampton Lectures, 1954 (London: A. R. Mowbray, 1954). Our representation of matters accords with Turner's chapter "Orthodoxy and the Bible" (241ff.).

2. Turner, *Pattern*, 258.

3. Ibid., 300.

A master of the Bavli could not have said it better in claiming both the systemic character and the traditional standing of his statement.

Let us hasten to qualify the comparison at hand. In claiming that a single problem, one of relating a system to tradition, for Judaism, or traditions into a system, for Christianity, found similar solutions in the Bavli and the Bible, we do not for one minute suggest that the two groups of intellectuals were thinking along the same lines. Quite to the contrary: the similarities were derived from different standpoints altogether. When the Christian theologians worked out the idea of "the Bible," consisting of "the Old Testament and the New Testament," and when the Judaic theologians worked out the idea of "the dual Torah," consisting of "the written Torah and the oral Torah," they may have been addressing a similar question; however, each party pursued the solution in a way that was particular to the internal logic and life of its own group.

True, as a matter of necessity, each party had to designate within the larger corpus of Scriptures coming from ancient Israel those writings that it regarded as authoritative and therefore as divinely revealed. But they did not do this for the same reasons and within the same sort of theological logic. Each party had further to explain to itself the end result, that is, the revealed words as a whole. The one party characterized the whole as a single book, a single piece of writing, the Bible; the other party characterized the whole as a single Torah, as revelation in two media: writing and memory. These characterizations of the result of revelation, that is, of the canon, hardly constitute intersecting statements.

As Turner testifies, in Christianity the process by which traditions became a system was governed by intention and a desired outcome; this process directly stemmed from the life of the Church, not from the issue of culture in its relationship to the logic of cogent discourse. Let us briefly review the formation of these received, traditional writings into a system — into, as Turner says, a canon, a pattern of Christian truth.

In the centuries after the Gospels were written, the Church had to come to a decision on whether, in addition to the Scriptures of ancient Israel, there would be a further corpus of authoritative writing. The Church affirmed that there would be, and the New Testament as counterpart to the Old Testament evolved into the canon. When we speak of canon, we refer, in Brevard Childs's words, to "the process of theological interpretation by a faith community [that] left its mark on a literary text which did not continue to evolve and which became the normative interpretation of the events to which it bore witness for those identifying with that religious community."[4]

Christians from the very beginning revered the Hebrew Scriptures as "the Old Testament," regarding it as their sacred book. They denied the Jews any claim to the book, accusing them of misinterpreting it. The Old Testament served, in Adolf Harnack's words, to prove "that the appearance and the entire history of Jesus had been predicted hundreds and even thousands of years ago; and further, that the founding of the New People which was to be fashioned out of all the nations upon earth had from the very beginning been prophesied and prepared for."[5] The text of the Hebrew Scriptures supplied proofs for various propositions of theology, law, and liturgy. It served as a source of precedents: "If God had praised or punished this or that in the past, how much more... are we to look for similar treatment from him, we who are now living in the last days and who have received 'the calling of promise.'"[6] Even after the rise of the New Testament, much of the Old Testament held its own. And, Harnack concludes, "The New Testament as a whole did not generally play the same role as the Old Testament in the mission and practice of the church."[7]

In the beginning the Church did not expect the canon — now meaning only the Hebrew Scriptures — to grow through Christian additions. As Frank M. Cross says, "In the new covenant the sole complement to the Word in the Torah was the Word made flesh in Christ."[8] So it would be some time before a Chris-

---

4. Brevard S. Childs, *The New Testament as Canon* (Valley Forge, Pa.: Trinity Press International, 1994, 1984), 26.

5. Adolf Harnack, *The Mission and Expansion of Christianity in the First Three Centuries* (New York: Harper & Brothers, 1962), 283.

6. Ibid., 284.

7. Ibid., 288.

8. Frank M. Cross, *Magnalia Dei: The Mighty Acts of God* (Garden City, N.Y.: Doubleday, 1976), 49.

tian canon encompassing not only the received writings but the writings of the new age would come into being. Before Marcion the Bible of the Church was the Hebrew Scriptures, pure and simple. Floyd Filson has concluded that the idea of a canon began to crystallize between the years 160 and 175 and that the process came to a halt by the end of the fourth century. Filson states that by that time "there was no longer any wide dispute over the right of any of our twenty-seven books to a place in the New Testament canon."[9] What was not a settled question for Eusebius, in 330, had been worked out by the last years of the fourth century.

So, in general, when we take up the issue of the canon of Christianity, we find ourselves in the third and fourth centuries.[10] The bulk of the work was complete by 200, with details under debate for another two hundred years.[11] The orthodoxy in which "the canon of an Old and a New Testament was firmly laid down" did not come into being overnight. From the time of Irenaeus the Church affirmed the bipartite Christian Bible, containing the Old Testament and, parallel with this and controlling it, the New Testament.[12] But what was to be in the New Testament, and when were the limits of the canon decided? Hans von Campenhausen concludes the description for us:

> [The Muratorian fragment] displays for the first time the concept of a collection of New Testament Scriptures, which has deliberately been closed, and the individual books of which are regarded as "accepted" and ecclesiastically "sanctified," that is to say...they have been "incorporated" into the valid corpus. We have thus arrived at the end of the long journey which leads to a New Testament thought of as "canonical" in the strict sense. Only one thing is still lacking: the precise name for this collection, which will make it possible to refer to the new Scripture as

---

9. Floyd Filson, *Which Books Belong in the Bible?* (Philadelphia: Westminster, 1957), 121.

10. Hans Von Campenhausen, *The Formation of the Christian Bible,* trans. A. Baker (London, 1972), 147; Filson, *Which Books,* 121.

11. Childs, *New Testament as Canon,* 18.

12. Von Campenhausen, *Formation,* 209.

a unity and thus at one and the same time both to distinguish it from the old Scriptures and combine it with them in a new totality.... This is the last feature still wanting to the accomplishment of the bipartite Christian Bible.[13]

When does the Old Testament join the New as the Bible? Von Campenhausen makes a striking point: there was no need to look for a single name for the entire document. There was no such thing as an Old Testament or a New Testament as a single physical entity. To the eye the whole canon was still fragmented into a series of separate rolls or volumes. Von Campenhausen makes a still more relevant point:

> There was no reason why in themselves the two parts of the Bible should not have different names. In the early period one possibility suggested itself almost automatically: if one had the New and the Old Testament in mind, one could speak of the "Gospel" and the "Law."[14]

The use of the terms "Old" and "New" Testament represents a particular theology. It was from the beginning of the third century that Scripture for orthodox Christianity consisted of an Old and a New Testament. Von Campenhausen concludes: "Both the Old and the New Testaments had in essence already reached their final form and significance around the year 200."[15] For Christianity, the authority of the Bible rested on the reliability of the predictions of Christ in the Prophets and on the apostles' testimony to Christ.[16] The biblical component of the "canon of truth" proved contingent, not absolute and dominant.

The Solutions Compared and Contrasted

We now realize that although the overall problem at issue was similar for Christianity and Judaism, the *specific* issues involved were in no way identical. None of the above-cited theological

---

13. Ibid., 261–62.
14. Ibid., 262.
15. Ibid., 327.
16. Ibid., 330.

precipitants for the canonical process played any role we can discern in the theory of the Torah in two media. The myth of the dual Torah, which functioned as a canonical process, validating as it did the writings of sages as part of the Torah from Sinai, derives neither from the analogy to the Old Testament process nor — to begin with — from the narrow issue of finding a place for the specific writings of rabbis within the larger Torah. It follows, then, that *we cannot refer to "the Bible" when we speak of Judaism.*[17]

When scholars of the formation of the canon of Christianity use the word "canon," they mean the following: (1) the recognition of sacred Scripture over and beyond the (received) Hebrew Scriptures; (2) the identification of writings revered within the Church as canonical, hence authoritative; (3) the recognition that these accepted writings formed a Scripture, which (4) served as the counterpart to the Hebrew Scriptures; hence

---

17. To state the matter simply: first comes the explanation of the place and role of the sage and his teachings; then comes the explanation of the place of the books that contain those teachings — in that order. We do not mean to ignore interesting debates on the canonization of the Christian Bible (the Old and the New Testaments). Childs (*New Testament,* 19) alerts us to issues that require further study: "[A]n important and highly debatable issue turns on determining the direction from which the New Testament canonical process proceeded. Did the canonization of the New Testament develop in analogy to an Old Testament process which had largely reached its goal of stabilization before the New Testament period, or rather did the major canonical force stem from the side of the Christian church, which resulted in the definition of the Jewish Scriptures as an Old Testament within the larger Christian Bible?" The answer to that question self-evidently does not affect our study.of the doctrine of the dual Torah of Sinai. The reason is that from the viewpoint of that doctrine, the question is meaningless. So Childs's quite proper question addresses the wrong category. The category is not the place of the teaching but of the teacher. In many ways the Montanist crisis turns on its head in Judaism. That is to say, sages held that they had every authority to teach Torah, then produced books that contained Torah from Sinai (beginning of course with the Mishnah). That is the message of Pirqé Abot. But by that theory Montanism is "right" and Orthodoxy wrong, so far as Montanism validates contemporary prophecy, hence, revelation by living persons — such as, within Judaism, sages. I hasten to apologize for venturing beyond my limits. These comments rely on the little I learned about Montanism in the secondary sources cited above, and I do not mean to offer a theory of the matter, only a contrast that seems suggestive. But I do mean to suggest that the process of canonization of the persons and authority of sages comes about through the myth of the dual Torah, and that process only later on also validates sages' principal documents — so showing us what the process of Christian canonization might have looked like had Montanism won.

(5) the formation of the Bible as the Old and New Testaments. Now, none of these categories, stage by stage, corresponds in any way to the processes in the unfolding of the holy books of the sages, which we describe in terms of Torah. In short, the word "Torah" in the context of the writings of the sages in no way forms a counterpart to the word "canon" as used (quite correctly) by Childs, von Campenhausen, and others; moreover, the word "Bible" and the word "Torah" in no way speak of the same thing; they do not refer to the same category or classification.

In fact the statement of the Bavli is not a canonical system at all, for in the mode of presentation of the Bavli's system, revelation does not close or reach conclusion. God speaks all the time through the sages. Representing the whole as "Torah" means that the Bavli speaks a tradition formed in God's revelation of God's will to Moses, our rabbi. Ancient Israel's Scriptures fall into the category of Torah, but they do not fill that category up. Other writings fall into that same category. The contrast, then, is this: "canon" refers to particular books that enjoy a distinctive standing; "Torah" refers to various things that fall into a particular classification. The Christian canon was closed. The Judaic Torah never closed — revelation of Torah continued.[18] The Torah is not the Bible, and the Bible is not the Torah. The Bible emerges within the larger process of establishing Church order and doctrine. The Torah (oral and written) derives from the larger process of working out the authority and standing of two successive and connected systems in relationship to the pentateuchal system.

A long-standing problem faced all system builders in the tradition that commenced with the Pentateuch. From that original system onward, system builders, both in Judaism and in Christianity, would have to represent their system not as an original statement on its own but as part of a tradition of revealed truth. In addition, but in the passage of time and in the accumulation of writing, intellectuals, both Christian and Judaic, would have to work out logics that would permit cogent discourse both

---

18. So too did the pattern of Christian truth, but in a different form and forum from the canonical Bible.

within the inherited traditions and with them. In the Christian case, the solution to the problem lay in accepting as canonical a variety of documents, each with its own logic. We note, for instance, that extraordinarily cogent communication could be accomplished, in most Christian writings, through symbol and not through proposition at all. Each Christian writing exhibits its own coherent logical principle of cogency, with the making of connections and the drawing of conclusions fully consistent throughout.

The final solution of the canon sidestepped the problem of bringing these logics together within a single statement. If diverse logics worked, each for its own authoritative writing, then there was no need, it was decided, to effect coherence among those logics at all, and the result of this was that the canon, the conception of the Bible, imposed from without a cogency of discourse difficult to discern in the interior of the canonical writings. That decision then dictated the future of the Christian intellectual enterprise: to explore the underbrush of the received writing and to straighten out the tangled roots. Centuries later, when the Christian mind became acquainted with Greek philosophy, the glories of logical and systematic order denied in a dictated canon would be recovered. But the canon did solve the problem that faced the heirs to a rather odd corpus of writing. Ignoring logic as of no account, accepting considerable diversity in modes of making connections and drawing conclusions, the traditional solution represented a better answer than the librarians of the Essenes at Qumran had found, which was (as far as we can now tell) to set forth neither a system nor a canon.

The Bavli's authors were the first in the history of Judaism, encompassing Christianity in its earliest phases,[19] to take up, in behalf of their distinct and distinctive system, a position of relationship with the received heritage of tradition, with a corpus of truth assigned to God's revelation to Moses at Sinai. The

---

19. We do not mean to ignore the school of Matthew and the numerous other Christian writers who cited proof texts for their propositions. But as we have seen in the case of their Judaic counterparts, merely citing proof texts is not the same thing as setting forth a complete system in the form of a tradition, such as was done by the Bavli's authors.

framers of the Pentateuch did not do so; rather they said what they wrote was the work of God, dictated to Moses at Sinai. The Essene librarians at Qumran did not do so. They collected this and that, never even pretending that everything fit together in some one way, not as commentary to Scripture (though some wrote commentaries), not as systemic statements (though the library included such statements, of course), and not as a canon (unless everything we find in the detritus forms a canon by definition). The authors of the Mishnah did not do so. Quite to the contrary, they undertook the pretense that, even when Scripture supplied facts and dictated the order of the facts, their writing was new and fresh and their own.[20] No wonder that the Mishnah's authors resorted to their own logic to make their own statement in their own language and for their own purposes.

No wonder, also, that the hubris of the Mishnah's authors provoked the systematic demonstration of the dependence of the Mishnah on Scripture — but also the allegation that the Mishnah stood as an autonomous statement, another Torah, the oral one, coequal with the written Torah. The hubris of the great intellects of Judaic and Christian antiquity, the daring authors of the Pentateuch and the Mishnah, the great ecclesiastical minds behind the Bible, reached its boldest realization in the Bavli. Through their ingenious joining of two distinct and contradictory logics of cogent discourse, these authors, as we have seen, formed the statement of the Torah in its own rhetoric, following its own logic, and in accord with its own designated topical program. But hubris is not the sole trait that characterizes the Jewish mind, encompassing its Christian successors, in classical times.

There is a second trait common to them all. It is that in all

---

20. The best example is M. Yoma, chapters 1 through 7, which follow the order of Leviticus 16 and review its rite, step-by-step, rarely citing the pertinent chapter of Scripture and never conceding that all that was in hand was a summary and paraphrase of rules available elsewhere. It is the simple fact that we cannot make any sense out of that tractate without a point-by-point consultation with Leviticus 16. There are numerous other examples in which the Mishnah's authors merely paraphrase passages of Scripture (along with many more in which Scripture has nothing to say on topics dealt with in the Mishnah, or in which what Scripture thinks important about a topic is simply ignored as of no interest in the Mishnah).

systemic constructions and statements the issues of logic responded to the systemic imperative and in no way dictated the shape and structure of that imperative. The system invariably proves to be prior, recapitulating itself, also, in its logic. And however diverse the issues addressed by various systems made up by the Jewish mind in classical times, all had to address a single question natural to the religious ecology in which Judaic systems flourished. That question, in the aftermath of the pentateuchal system, concerned how people could put together in a fresh construction and a composition of distinctive proportions a statement that purported to speak truth to a social entity that, in the nature of things, already had truth. This framing of the issue of how system contradicts tradition, how the logic that tells me to make a connection of this to that, but not to the other thing, and to draw from that connection one conclusion, rather than some other — that framing of the issue places intellect, the formation of mind and modes of thought, squarely into the ongoing processes dictated by the givens of society.

Why then characterize the Bavli's system builders as the climax of the hubris of the Jewish intellectuals? Because (as we have said) the Bavli's authors were the first in the history of Judaism, encompassing Christianity in its earliest phases, to take up, in behalf of their distinct and distinctive system, a position of relationship with the received heritage of tradition, with a corpus of truth assigned to God's revelation to Moses at Sinai. Four centuries after the Mishnah, in their mind eighteen centuries after God revealed the Torah to Moses at Mount Sinai, the Bavli's authors remade the two received systems, the pentateuchal and the mishnaic. In their own rhetoric, in accord with their own topical program, appealing to a logic unique to themselves among all Jewish minds in ancient times, these authors presented the Torah of Sinai precisely as they wished to represent it. And they did so defiantly, not discreetly nor by indirection.

Not merely alleging that Moses had written the entire Torah down, like the pentateuchal compilers, nor modestly identifying with the direction of the Holy Spirit the choices that it made, like the Christians responsible for making the Bible, nor even, as with the framers of the Mishnah, sedulously sidestepping, in laconic and disingenuous innocence, the issue of authority and tradition entirely, the Bavli's intellectuals took over the entire tradition, scriptural and mishnaic alike, chose what they wanted, tacked on to the selected passages their own words in their own way, and then put it all out as a single statement of their own.

True, they claimed for their system the standing of a mere amplification of that tradition. But, as a matter of fact, they did say it all in their own words, and they did set forth the whole of their statement in their own way and — above all — without capitulating to the received choices of ignoring or merely absorbing the received revelation; they represented as the one whole Torah revealed by God to Moses, our rabbi, at Sinai what they themselves had made up, and they made it stick. And that, we think, is the supreme hubris of the Jewish mind from the beginnings, in the Pentateuch, to the conclusion and climax in the Bavli. We like to think that that hubris of theirs at least for the beauty of it explains the success of what they made up, on the simple principle, the more daring, the more plausible. For theirs was the final realization and statement in the formation of the Jewish intellect. Their mode of making connections and drawing conclusions defined, from then to now, the systems and the traditions of Judaism.

Part One

Knowing God in the Torah

JACOB NEUSNER

How We Know God:
The Torah, Written and Oral

The Torah and the Theology of Judaism

The origin of Judaism, the religion, is God's revelation of the Torah to Moses at Mount Sinai, and the purpose of Judaism is living in accord with the covenant God made with holy Israel, the people, through the Torah at Sinai. Judaism's purpose, then, is to know God through the Torah.

We have used two kinds of terms in this statement: "Judaism" is descriptive, and "the Torah" is native. Although the terms point to separate categories, they refer to the same thing. That is to say, although the former speaks *about* the faith and the latter speaks *within* it, the terms coincide. Both terms refer to a way to God and to the love and service of God that have been chosen by "Israel," a word that here designates not the contemporary state of Israel, or indeed any political or ethnic entity, but rather the holy people — a kingdom of priests and a holy nation — to which the Hebrew Scriptures refer. People who today regard themselves as heirs to the Israel of which Scripture speaks, and who believe that in the Torah they know God, practice the religion that the world knows as Judaism.

Two sentences that say the same thing show what is at stake in the distinction between the descriptive and the native:

1. The secular, *descriptive* sentence: "Rigorous, sustained reflection upon revelation forms the theology of Judaism."

2. The sentence employing *native* language: "Study of the Torah as the Talmud presents the Torah teaches us the will of God."

The two words "Judaism" and "Torah" are correlative, but each imposes its own logic and discipline. That is, according to the secular language of the West, Judaism is the whole, complete, authoritative, fully composed religion, with its system comprising a way of life, worldview, and theory of the social entity, Israel; according to the theological language of the faith, that same whole, complete, and authoritative entity is what the Torah presents. At stake, then, is the way in which we perceive and understand that entity.

"The theology of Judaism" as it came to full and systematic expression in its authoritative document requires an inquiry into the nature and structure of the Torah. The inquiry into nature and structure encompasses the media designated with the status of Torah: that is, the persons, books, gestures, hierarchical authority in the social order, and modes of thought and expression that fall into the category Torah and require orderly systematization as a single, coherent statement. There is, however, a redundancy at work here: the statement "The theology of Judaism comes to realization in the Torah" is redundant because "theology of Judaism" in one language of thought is the same as "the Torah" in the other. And both "theology of Judaism" and "the Torah" cover the same ground in a deeper sense, since each promises the same thing as the other: knowledge of God and God's will for humanity.

But what is it about God that is made manifest in the Torah? We know the mind of God through the intellection — the modes of thought, the attitudes, the ways of reasoned communication — exemplified in the Torah. That means, what defines humanity and what defines God, in rationality, is the same thing: we are consubstantial in mind. It follows that, first, the category "Torah" defines the theology of Judaism, and, second, knowledge of the Torah tells us how God thinks. We shall now see that these statements are natural — fully native — to the documents of Judaism. In light of what was said in the introduction, readers will not be surprised at our turning immediately to the Talmud of Babylonia, the full, complete, and authoritative representation of the Torah as holy Israel receives it day by day.

We begin with a concrete example of the extent to which that single category, the Torah, overspreads the social order, intellect, and hierarchy alike, governing conduct and conviction in all details. Examples such as this show how correct conduct and conviction form "torah" as authoritative propositions and governing rules and come to formulation in "the Torah." Texts such as these dictate correct usage, right action and doctrine, matters of status, position, the arrangement of the social order, and on upward to who may marry whom. Proper speech and proper conduct find entire definition in the Torah, and errors in the one or the other indicate a person is not a master of the Torah and so is not reliable. The following story shows us the range of what is at issue when we speak of "torah" or "the Torah":

5.   A. There was a man from Nehardea who went into a butchershop in Pumbedita. He said to them, "Give me meat."

     B. They said to him, "Wait until the servant of R. Judah bar Ezekiel gets his, and then we'll give to you."

     C. He said, "So who is this Judah bar Sheviskel who comes before me to get served before me?"

     D. They went and told R. Judah.

     E. He excommunicated him.

     F. They said, "He is in the habit of calling people slaves."

     G. He proclaimed concerning him, "He is a slave."

     H. The other party went and sued him in court before R. Nahman.

     I. When the summons came, R. Judah went to R. Huna and said to him, "Should I go, or shouldn't I go?"

     J. He said to him, "In point of fact, you really don't have to go, because you are an eminent authority. But on account of the honor owing to the household of the patriarch [of the Babylonian Jews], get up and go."

     K. He came. He found him [i.e., R. Nahman] making a parapet.

     L. He said to him, "Doesn't the master concur with what R. Huna bar Idi said Samuel said, 'Once a man is appointed administrator of the community, it is forbidden for him to do servile labor before three persons'?"

M. He said to him, "I'm just making a little piece of the balustrade."

N. He said to him, "So what's so bad about the word 'parapet,' which the Torah uses, or the word 'partition,' which rabbis use?"

O. He said to him, "Will the master sit down on a seat?"

P. He said to him, "So what's so bad about 'chair,' which rabbis use, or the word 'stool,' which people generally use?"

Q. He said to him, "Will the master eat a piece of citron-fruit?"

R. He said to him, "This is what Samuel said, 'Whoever uses the word 'citron-fruit' is a third puffed up with pride.' It should be called either etrog, as the rabbis do, or 'lemony-thing,' as people do."

S. He said to him, "Would the master like to drink a goblet of wine?"

T. He said to him, "So what's so bad about the word 'wine-glass,' as rabbis say, or 'a drink,' as people say?"

U. He said to him, "Let my daughter Dunag bring something to drink."

V. He said to him, "This is what Samuel said, 'People are not to make use of a woman.'"

W. "But she's only a minor!"

X. "In so many words said Samuel, 'People are not to make use of a woman in any manner, whether adult or minor.'"

Y. "Would the master care to send a greeting to my wife, Yalta?"

Z. He said to him, "This is what Samuel said, 'Even the sound of a woman's voice is [forbidden as] lustful.'"

AA. "Maybe through a messenger?"

BB. He said to him, "This is what Samuel said [70B], 'People are not to inquire after a woman's health.'"

CC. "Through her husband?!"

DD. He said to him, "This is what Samuel said, 'People are not to inquire after a woman's health in any way, shape, or form.'"

EE. His wife sent word to him, "Settle the man's case for him, so that he not make you like any other fool."

FF. He said to him, "So what brings you here?"

GG. He said to him, "You sent me a subpoena." He said to him, "Now if even the language of the master I don't know, how in the world could I have sent you a subpoena?!"

HH. He produced the summons from his bosom and showed it to him: "Here is the man, here is the subpoena!"

II. He said to him, "Well, anyhow, since the master has come here, let's discuss the matter, so people should not say that rabbis are showing favoritism to one another."

JJ. He said to him, "How come the master has excommunicated that man?" "He harassed a messenger of the rabbis."

KK. "So why didn't the master flog him, for Rab would flog someone who harassed a messenger of the rabbis."

LL. "I did worse to him."

MM. "How come the master declared the man a slave?"

NN. "Because he went around calling other people slaves, and there is a Tannaite statement: Whoever alleges that others are genealogically invalid is himself invalid and never says a good thing about other people. And said Samuel, 'By reference to a flaw in himself he invalidates others.'"

OO. "Well, I can concede that Samuel said to suspect such a man of such a genealogy, but did he really say to make a public declaration to that effect? ... " (B. Qidd. 70A–B)

The category "Torah" enters this story at a number of distinct points. First, the master of Torah is accorded authority and honor; when he is not, he will exclude the other party from "Israel," placing him into ostracism ("excommunication") or assigning him to a social status as a slave, which prevents him from marrying into "Israel." Second, the master of Torah conducts himself properly. He signifies his status by using one word, rather than some other word, for common objects. He accomplishes the same goal also by the manner of his conduct with women. It goes without saying that sages not only act impartially but make certain they are seen to act impartially.

It follows that if we wish to know how this religious system speaks and what it wishes to say, we have to listen to what it says in the Torah and how it makes that statement. Here we see in strikingly concrete ways how "the Torah" defines the world-view and the way of life of holy Israel; the most common details of conduct are infused with transcendental consequence.

Before we can approach the more profound issue, how the Torah gives us access to God's rationality, we have to take a roundabout route. First, in order to speak intelligibly we have to utilize our categories, so that defining the task in overlapping languages — the secular language of Western learning, the religious language of "Judaism" or "the Torah" — is required. The reason is simple. It is the only way we can formulate what is required to accomplish our task of theological description, analysis, and interpretation in a determinate historical setting. So both languages — the language of the academy, speaking of "Judaism" or "theology," and the language of the native category, speaking of "torah" and "the Torah" — are necessary. The language of the academy of the West shapes our intellect and forms our organizing categories and our analytical tool; without it, all we do is paraphrase our sources. The language of the academy of Judaism, the *yeshiva*, provides access to our sources and defines the subject and system that we study; without it, we generalize without data and describe what we have not, in fact, examined at all.

A restatement of matters using the two functionally equivalent word formations ("Judaism" or "Torah") shows us what is at stake. Since in the authentic speech of Judaism "the Torah is given by God to Moses at Sinai," a statement of theological and not historical consequence, it must follow that any grasp of the theology of Judaism (in the intelligible speech of our own modes of thought and expression) must begin with an understanding of how the Torah is mediated and comes to mature expression (in language suitable to both Judaism and contemporary sensibility). We can frame this in two statements:

1. Speaking our langauge, we invoke the category "the theology of Judaism";

2. Speaking also the language of the faith of the Torah, we talk about torah (status, method, authority) and the Torah (substance, message, truth) in the language of the documents of the Torah, which is to say, the canonical writings of the Judaism of the dual Torah, written and oral.

To accomplish the purpose of definition, therefore, matters are stated in the two languages at once. This can be stated in a tripartite formulation:

1. Judaism states its theology through

2. the language and in the propositions of the Torah. Since Judaism is classified as a religion among religions, the statement "Judaism states its theology" addresses the matter of what we know of God and how we know it, to begin with. The reason is that

3. at stake in the Torah — for the religion of the Torah that is called Judaism — is knowledge of God.

Then the entire theology of Judaism may be expressed in the language of the Torah in a formulation that accommodates both Western, academic language and the forms of speech of the Torah; it is through the Torah — God's own manifestation to Moses and holy Israel, and God's self-manifestation — that faithful Israel knows God.

Now let me state the theology of Judaism in the language of the Torah, once more joining the two categories, native and secular. The Torah is the sole medium of God's revelation; it bears the unique message of God; and the Torah also conveys the correct method for the inquiry into the medium in quest of the truthful message: all three. Through learning in the Torah we know God.

These statements, setting forth as generalizations of a descriptive character the generative convictions of the Torah, that is, "Judaism," are unique to Judaism. The reason is not only the "context-specific" usage, "the Torah." It is more general. No other religion can make them. These authoritative statements of the Torah/Judaism exclude much else that in other religions is commonly thought to afford knowledge of God; the two most common and paramount are knowledge of God through nature and history. In the Torah, God is made known not through nature on its own, nor through history uninterpreted, but through nature set forth by the Torah as God's creation ("In the beginning God created..."; "The heavens declare the glory of God"), through history as explained through the Torah as a work of God's will ("You have seen how I..."). So we recover our starting point to define the term "theology"; knowing God defines the work of the theology of Judaism, or, to phrase matters in the native category and its language once more, through the Torah Israel meets God.

We may then identify the theology of this Judaism with the following formulation: "All our knowledge of divine truth... depends on God's prior self-manifestation; there is no knowledge of God unless he reveals and we reason."[1] This formulation of contemporary philosophical theology in correct, academic language accurately and completely describes the entire program of the theology of Judaism. It is hardly necessary once more to translate it into the language of Judaism, but an appropriate counterpart language for the same position may be identified in the liturgical setting when the Torah is proclaimed to faithful Israel at worship: "Blessed are you, Lord, our God, who has chosen us from among all nations by giving us the Torah. Blessed are you, who gives the Torah," and, at the end, "Blessed are you, Lord, our God, who has given us the true Torah and so planted within us life eternal. Blessed are you, who gives the Torah." When we know how through the Torah Israel knows God, we know the theology of Judaism. And then, about God there is nothing more to be known.

The Torah and God's Intellect

We now come to the second point, namely, how the Torah reveals God's intellect and ours as well. What, exactly, is to be known about God in the theology of Judaism, or, phrasing the

---

1. Ingolf Dalferth, "The Stuff of Revelation: Austin Farrer's Doctrine of Inspired Images," in *Hermeneutics, the Bible and Literary Criticism,* ed. Ann Loades and Michael McLain (London: Macmillan, 1992), 71.

question in the native category: "What does the Torah say about the Holy One, blessed be he?" Obviously its messages are many, from an account of attributes ("The Lord, the Lord is merciful and long-suffering"), to the story of immediate encounter ("You shall not see my face"; "...the thin voice of silence"), and, above all, to the detailed and insistent account of what God commands Israel and covenants himself to do in regard to Israel. That, after all, is the principal message of the Torah par excellence. But the Torah not only sets forth propositions — things God is, has done, or wants of us. "Our sages of blessed memory" notice that the Torah also lays out sentences God has said. Since through language we reveal not only what is on and in our minds but also the very working of our minds, through the language of the Torah we gain access to God's mind. Humanity is like God specifically in intellect: God and the human being are joined in a common rationality.

A single, representative text serves to show that this view comes to expression not only implicitly but in every line of the Torah. It is stated in so many words in a story embedded in the Talmud itself, one that says quite explicitly that in heaven the Torah is studied in accord with the same rules of rationality as on earth, so that in heaven, as much as on earth, the intervention of the sage is required. God is bound by the same rules of reasoning as the sage; a common rationality governs; the Torah contains that truth of utter integrity. The fact that this conviction is made articulate entirely validates this representation of matters. We examine the bulk of the story to show the broader context in which it is taken for granted that God and the sage think in the same way about the same things. Not only so, but the same rules that govern on earth, dictate right thinking in heaven as well, and God is bound by those rules. That is because God made them to begin with and made humanity in conformity with them. The first section shows that God and the sage think in the same way about the same things:

A. Said R. Kahana, "R. Hama, son of the daughter of Hassa, told me that Rabbah b. Nahmani died in a persecution. [And here is the story:]

B. "Snitches squealed on him to the government, saying, 'There is a man among the Jews who keeps twelve thousand Israelites from paying the royal poll tax for a month in the summer and for a month in the winter.' [This Rabbah did by conducting huge public lectures, keeping people away from home, where they were counted for the poll tax.]

C. "They sent a royal investigator [*parastak*] for him, but he did not find him. He fled, going from Pumbedita to Aqra, from Aqra to Agma, from Agma to Shehin, from Shehin to Seripa, from Seripa to Ena Damim, from Ena Damim back to Pumbedita. In Pumbedita he found him.

D. "The royal investigator happened by the inn where Rabbah was located. They brought him [the detective] two glasses of liquor and then took away the tray [and this excited the ill-will of demons]. His face was turned backward. They said to him, 'What shall we do with him? He is the king's man.'

E. "[Rabbah] said to them, 'Bring him [the detective] the tray again, and let him drink another cup, and then remove the tray, and he will get better.'

F. "They did just that, and he got better.

G. "He [the detective] said, 'I am sure that the man whom I am hunting is here.' He looked for him and found him.

H. "He [the sage] said, 'I'm leaving here. If I am killed, I won't reveal a thing, but if they torture me, I'm going to squeal.'

I. "They brought him [the sage] to him [the detective] and he [the detective] put him [the sage] in a room and locked the door on him. But [Rabbah] sought mercy, the wall fell down, and he fled to Agma. He was in session on the trunk of a palm and studying.

J. "Now in the session in the firmament they were debating the following subject: if the bright spot preceded the white hair, he is unclean, and if the white hair preceded the bright spot, he is clean. [The Mishnah paragraph continues: And if it is a matter of doubt, he is unclean. And R. Joshua was in doubt.] [M. Neg. 4:11F–H]

K. "The Holy One, blessed be he, says, 'It is clean.'

L. "And the entire session in the firmament says, 'Unclean.' [We see, therefore, that in heaven, Mishnah study was going forward, with the Holy One participating and setting forth his ruling, as against the consensus of the other sages of the Torah in heaven.]

M. "They said, 'Who is going to settle the question? It is Rabbah bar Nahmani.'

N. "For said Rabbah bar Nahmani, 'I am absolutely unique in my knowledge of the marks of skin disease that is unclean and in the rules of uncleanness having to do with the corpse in the tent.'

O. "They sent an angel for him, but the angel of death could not draw near to him, since his mouth did not desist from repeating his learning. But in the meanwhile a wind blew and caused a rustling in the bushes, so he thought it was a troop of soldiers. He said, 'Let me die but not be handed over to the kingdom.'

P. "When he was dying, he said, 'It is clean, it is clean.' An echo came forth and said, 'Happy are you, Rabbah bar Nahmani, that your body is clean, and your soul has come forth in cleanness.' [The body would not putrefy.]

Q. "A note fell down from heaven in Pumbedita: 'Rabbah bar Nahmani has been invited to the session that is on high.'

R. "Abayye, Raba, and all the rabbis came forth to tend to his corpse, but they did not know where he was located. They went to Agma and saw birds [vultures] hovering over and overshadowing the corpse. 'This proves that he is there.'

S. "They mourned him for three days and three nights. A note fell down: 'Whoever refrains [from the mourning] will be excommunicated.' They mourned for him for seven days. A note fell down: 'Go now to your homes in peace.'

T. "The day on which he died a strong wind lifted a Tai-Arab who was riding on a camel from one side of the Pappa canal and threw him down onto the other side. He said, 'What is this?'

U. "They told him, 'Rabbah bar Nahmani has died.'

V. "He said before him, 'Lord of the world, the whole world is yours, and Rabbah bar Nahmani is yours. You are Rabbah's, and Rabbah is yours. Why are you destroying the world on his account?' The wind subsided." (B. B. Mes. 86A)

The critical point in this story comes at three places. First, God and the sages in heaven study the Torah in the same way as the Torah is studied on earth. Second, God is bound by the same rules of rationality as prevail down here. Third, the sage on earth studies the way God does in heaven, and God calls up to heaven for sages whose exceptional acuity and perspicacity are required on the occasion. It follows that our processes of analytical reasoning — when rightly carried out — can replicate God's: that is, we can think like God and in that way be holy like God. This statement merely paraphrases in abstract language precisely the point on which this and other stories rest.

Now, we must proceed to consider why and how rules reveal the mind of God. We begin with the implicit proposition of the foregoing: God is bound by the same rules of logical analysis and sound discourse that govern sages. Readers may suppose that this conclusion is compelled only by the logic of the system, perhaps also by implicit traits of some of the documents. But the view is stated explicitly as well. In the following story we find an explicit affirmation of the priority of reasoned argument over all other forms of discovery of truth:

II.1.A. There we have learned: if one cut [a clay oven] into parts and put sand between the parts,

    B. R. Eliezer declares the oven broken down and therefore insusceptible to uncleanness.

    C. And sages declare it susceptible to uncleanness.

    D. And this is what is meant by the oven of Akhnai. [M. Kel. 5:10].

    E. Why [is it called] the oven of Akhnai?

    F. Said R. Judah said Samuel, "It is because they surrounded it with argument as with a snake and proved it was insusceptible to uncleanness."

2. A. It has been taught on Tannaite authority:

    B. On that day R. Eliezer produced all of the arguments in the world, but they did not accept them from him. So he said to them, "If the law accords with my position, this carob tree will prove it."

    C. The carob was uprooted from its place by a hundred cubits — and some say, four hundred cubits.

D. They said to him, "There is no proof from a carob tree."

E. So he went and said to them, "If the law accords with my position, let the stream of water prove it."

F. The stream of water reversed flow.

G. They said to him, "There is no proof from a stream of water."

H. So he went and said to them, "If the law accords with my position, let the walls of the schoolhouse prove it."

I. The walls of the schoolhouse tilted toward falling.

J. R. Joshua rebuked them, saying to them, "If disciples of sages are contending with one another in matters of law, what business do you have?"

K. They did not fall on account of the honor owing to R. Joshua, but they also did not straighten up on account of the honor owing to R. Eliezer, and to this day they are still tilted.

L. So he went and said to them, "If the law accords with my position, let the heaven prove it!"

M. An echo came forth, saying, "What business have you with R. Eliezer, for the law accords with his position under all circumstances!"

N. R. Joshua stood up on his feet and said, " 'It is not in heaven' (Deut. 30:12)."

3. A. What is the sense of, " 'It is not in heaven' (Deut. 30:12)"?

B. Said R. Jeremiah, "[The sense of Joshua's statement is this:] For the Torah has already been given from Mount Sinai, so we do not pay attention to echoes, since you have already written in the Torah at Mount Sinai, 'After the majority you are to incline' (Exod. 23:2)."

4. A. R. Nathan came upon Elijah and said to him, "What did the Holy One, blessed be he, do at that moment?"

B. He said to him, "He laughed and said, 'My children have overcome me, my children have overcome me!' " (B. B. Mes. 59A–B).

The testimony of nature is null. The (mere) declaration of matters by heaven is dismissed. Sages now possess the Torah, and sages master the Torah through logical argument, right reason-

ing, the give-and-take of proposition and refutation, argument
and counterargument, and evidence arrayed in accord with the
rules of proper analysis. Then the majority will be persuaded,
one way or the other, entirely by sound argument: and the
majority prevails on that account.

So when heaven sends for Rabbah, it is because Rabbah
stands for a capacity that heaven as much as sages require; if
God rejoices at the victory in the give-and-take of argument of
the sages, it is because God is subject to the same rules of argument, evidence, and analysis. Therefore, if we want to know
God, we shall find God in the Torah: not in what the Torah says
alone, but in how the Torah reaches conclusions; this refers not
to the process of argument but to the principles of thought. God
has revealed the latter in the Torah, and in them we encounter
God's own intellect. This is why the theology of Judaism sets
forth knowledge of God as God is made known through God's
self-revelation in the Torah.

It follows that the Torah reveals not only what God wants of
humanity through Israel but what humanity can know of what
God is. The being of God that is revealed in the Torah — by the
nature of that medium of revelation, the Torah itself, made up
of words we know and sentences we can understand and forming connections we can follow and replicate — is God's will and
intellect. Within the religion of the Torah, therefore, there is ample occasion to take up the labor of learning not only what but
how God thinks. What is at stake in that lesson is how we too
should conduct intellection. And the upshot will be, if we think
the way we should, that we may enter deep into the processes
of the Torah and so reach propositions in the way in which God
has thought things through too. The theology of Judaism provides an account of what it means to know God through the
Torah (a sentence that is made up of two equivalent and redundant clauses: [1] "theology of Judaism proves..." and [2] "know
God through the Torah"). What makes that theology interesting
is its special sense of what knowing God through the Torah involves, requires, and affords: knowing what it means rightly to
know. Three steps lead to that simple conclusion.

First, knowing God and striving to be holy like God ("Let
us make man in our image...after our likeness"; "You shall be

holy, for I the Lord your God am holy") define the lessons of the Torah or "Judaism."

Second, this knowledge is both unique and sufficient; it is only through the Torah that knowledge of God comes to humanity. The Torah comes to Israel in particular because of God's decision and choice. God gave the Torah, or, in the language of liturgy, "... gives the Torah."

Third, knowledge of God depends not only on God's self-revelation through the Torah. It requires also humanity's — therefore, uniquely, Israel's — proper grasp of the Torah. And this requires active engagement: sagacity, wit, erudition, and intelligence. Gifts of intellect form instruments of grace: elements of God's self-revelation. The reason is that by thinking about thought as much as thinking thoughts, we ask the deeper question about what we can know about God, which is, God's thoughts in God's words, which, rightly grasped, expose God's thought.

Proper inquiry after God in the Torah therefore requires sound method, that is, right questions, proper modes of analysis, reliable use of probative evidence, and compelling reasoning. These are media of revelation accessible to humanity through the Torah (in its oral as much as in its written components) and its everywhere-unitary rules of reasoning. For the Torah comes to Israel in the medium of language, some of it written down right away, at Sinai, some of it orally formulated and transmitted and only later on written down. Knowledge of God comes not through the silence of wordless sentiment or inchoate encounter in unarticulated experience, or through the thin voice of silence alone, a silence without words. Knowledge of God reaches us solely through the reflection afterward on what has been felt or thought or said by the voice of silence.

Modes of bringing knowledge of God into the form of language began with the writing down of the Torah itself, which for Israel records not only God's will but the actual words God used in stating that will to Moses, our rabbi. Therefore, knowledge of the grammar and syntax of God's thought is learned through mastery of reading the Torah's words themselves — which words pertain here, which there, and what conclusions to draw about God, on the one side, and what humanity embodied in Israel, on the other. The authentic theologians of Judaism, then, are our sages of blessed memory who know how and why to read the Torah.

This religious system reaches its statement in documents, even though, as we have already seen in the story about right conduct with women and right word choices, other media besides closed writings serve the same purpose. Still, the principal statement is made by a single, formidable, sustained writing that — now speaking in description and fact — from the time of its closure to our own day made and now makes the summary statement of Judaism and defines the curriculum in centers where people study the Torah. This sustained, systematic exposition, through one instance after another, of the right reading of the Torah in both its media comes to Israel now as in the past in a single document, the Talmud of Babylonia.

The Talmud of Babylonia

The Talmud has been central in the curriculum of the Judaic intellect and has held priority from the time of its closure around 600 C.E. to the present time. The Talmud is the prism, receiving and refracting all light. To state the proposition in academic language: into that writing all prior canonical (that is, authoritative) documents flowed; from it, all later canonical writings emerged; to it all appeal is directed; upon it, all conclusions ultimately rest. Now in the language of the Torah itself: study of the Torah begins, as a matter of simple, ubiquitous fact, in the Talmud.

Proof of these simple propositions on the talmudic representation of the Torah, which is to say, Judaism's statement of its theology, of its norms of action and reflection, and of the authority that sustains them and signifies right from wrong, derives from the character of Judaic discourse. In all times, places, and writings, other than those rejected as heretical, from then to now, the Talmud formed the starting point and the ending point, the alpha and omega, of truth; justify by appeal to the Talmud, rightly read, persuasively interpreted, and you make your point; disprove a proposition by reference to a statement of the Talmud, and you demolish a counterpoint. In reading the written Torah itself, the Talmud's exegesis enjoys priority of place. Scripture rightly read reaches Israel in the Talmud (and related writings of Midrash); sound exegesis conforms to the facts of the Talmud (and Midrash) or can be shown, at least, not to be out of line with them. Even greater consequence attaches to action. In all decisions of law that express theology in everyday action, the Talmud forms the final statement of the Torah, mediating Scripture's rules.

Innovation of every kind, whether in the character of the spiritual life or in the practice of the faith in accord with its norms, must find justification in the Talmud, however diverse the means by which validation is accomplished. The schools and courts of the holy community of Israel studied the Torah in the Talmud and applied its laws. The faithful emulated masters of the Torah in the Talmud and accepted their instruction. Even in modern times those systems acknowledge the authority of the Talmud. For instance, in modern times the self-segregation of "the people that dwells apart" was rejected, and Judaic systems took shape that intended to integrate holy Israel into the common life of the nations where Jews lived. This proposed profound change in the social policy of holy Israel appealed to the Talmud's norms. The proposal could not have prevailed unless the Talmud could be shown to approve of the change. Both sides recognized the issue — and therefore affirmed the authority of the document.

The premise is then shown to generate yet another principle, which reaches upward into other cases that lie in a different terrain altogether. The cases presuppose contrary principles, and the principles express conflicting premises. Thus the disharmony demands detailed attention, a work of harmonization not of detail nor yet of principle but of the most abstract formulations of premise. Right reasoning and its rules hold the whole together.

To what end? Clearly, knowing how to decipher the signals of dialogue allows us to come to conclusions but, more to the point, even to re-create an argument, one that would lead from out here, in the real world of cases and examples, inward, into the profound reaches of the Torah, where at the deepest struc-

ture we grasp what we can of God's will and intellect. The
Talmud makes it possible to replicate the modes of thought that
yielded principles and rules. The Torah then forms the data out
of which we may find in the layers of abstraction and generalization the rules of reasoned reality: the world attests to the
intent and mind of its Maker. The integrity, unity, and coherence of truth are traits of intellect that attest to God's mind,
from which all things come, to which all things refer. The rules
of life therefore came to this-worldly expression within the
Torah, and to those with wit and patience those rules would
be fully exposed in all their unity and integrity by the Torah.

So the stakes of the second Talmud prove formidable indeed.
This is why the theology of Judaism (in academic language)
forms a statement of what it means to know God; and that
theology defines what it means to know God in terms both particular but wholly accessible to the mind of all creation endowed
with sensibility. God is wholly other, but God has given the
Torah, thus revealing to holy Israel both the terms of endear-
ment — what God wants of Israel — and also the appropriate
terminology, or, the how and the why behind the what.

Above all the Torah defines all relationships, how God loves
humanity, and how humanity is to respond in deed and de-
liberation. Therefore, the Torah comes to Israel in an encounter
("dialogue"), first between Moses and God and then between
the disciple and the master, which replicates the relationship
between Moses and God. It follows that the critical moment
comes at the encounter of master and disciple, where, here and
now, both enter into the situation of God and Moses.

This conception of relationship reaches definition in three
ways: concrete, abstract, and mythic. First, the concrete rule:

I.   A. [If he has to choose between seeking] what he has lost and
         what his father has lost,

     B. his own takes precedence.

II. C. [If he has to choose between seeking] what he has lost and
         what his master has lost,

     D. his own takes precedence.

E. [If he has to choose between seeking] what his father has lost and what his master has lost, that of his master takes precedence.

F. For his father brought him into this world.

G. But his master, who taught him wisdom, will bring him into the life of the world to come.

H. But if his father is a sage, that of his father takes precedence.
(M. B. Mes. 2:11)

Now the abstract statement of the theological fact:

A. Moses received the Torah at Sinai and handed it on to Joshua, Joshua to elders, and elders to prophets. And prophets handed it on to the men of the great assembly. They said three things: Be prudent in judgment. Raise up many disciples. Make a fence for the Torah. (M. Abot 1:1)

Third, the explicit mythic formulation of how the relationship of master to disciple replicates the relationship between God and Moses:

A. Our rabbis have taught on Tannaite authority:

B. What is the order of Mishnah teaching? Moses learned it from the mouth of the All-Powerful. Aaron came in, and Moses repeated his chapter to him, and Aaron went forth and sat at the left hand of Moses. His sons came in, and Moses repeated their chapter to them, and his sons went forth. Eleazar sat at the right of Moses, and Itamar at the left of Aaron.

C. R. Judah says, "At all times Aaron was at the right hand of Moses."

D. Then the elders entered, and Moses repeated for them their Mishnah chapter. The elders went out. Then the whole people came in, and Moses repeated for them their Mishnah chapter. So it came about that Aaron repeated the lesson four times, his sons three times, the elders two times, and all the people once.

E. Then Moses went out, and Aaron repeated his chapter for them. Aaron went out. His sons repeated their chapter. His sons went out. The elders repeated their chapter. So it turned out that everybody repeated the same chapter four times. (B. Erub. 54B)

We conclude with yet another concrete formulation of the theology in terms of everyday rules of conduct:

F. On this basis said R. Eliezer, "A person is liable to repeat the lesson for his disciple four times. And it is an argument a fortiori: if Aaron, who studied from Moses himself, and Moses from the Almighty — so in the case of a common person who is studying with a common person, all the more so!"

G. R. Aqiba says, "How on the basis of Scripture do we know that a person is obligated to repeat a lesson for his disciple until he learns it [however many times that takes]? As it is said, 'And you teach it to the children of Israel' (Deut. 31:19). And how do we know that that is until it will be well ordered in their mouth? 'Put it in their mouths' (Deut. 31:19). And how on the basis of Scripture do we know that he is liable to explain the various aspects of the matter? 'Now these are the ordinances which you shall put before them' (Exod. 31:1)." (B. Erub. 54B)

We see, therefore, what is at stake in the Talmud, its study in the right way, its transmission in the proper manner — namely, knowledge of God, such as God makes manifest through the Torah. And this is the only knowledge of God that Judaism maintains we have.

Accessible only in the living encounter, at the Torah, of the master and the disciple, the Talmud set forth the Torah as Israel received — and now receives — it night and morning through all time. What the abstract statement means in concrete terms then is simple. In reconstructing its arguments, analyzing its initiatives of proposition and objection, argument and counterargument, thrust and parry, movement of thought and momentum of mind, the Talmud's disciples formed their minds and framed their modes of thought in the encounter with the Torah. And, in making up their own statements, the best of them could therefore claim (though none of them ever did) to think the way God thought about the things about which God thinks: the rules of life as set forth in the Torah.

In the history of all Judaic systems that appealed to the same Scripture — the written Torah or Pentateuch or, indeed, the entirety of the Scriptures that people call "the Old Testament" — the Talmud of Babylonia is an utterly unique document. The Judaism that found definition in that writing, the system that came to expression therein, has no counterpart in any other of the Judaisms of all times and places. Take the simple but fundamental matter of how the Torah (that is, "Judaism") is set forth. All other Judaisms made their statement in declarative sentences and defined their systemic messages solely in propositions. This Judaism insisted on exposing the how, not only the what, of thought. Whatever any other Judaism chose to say, its authors spelled it out in so many words. This Judaism insists the faithful participate in the discovery of the norm and understand the modes of rationality that come to expression in the norm.

For every other Judaism, as a matter of simple, descriptive fact, the content of the Torah or of tradition was wholly doctrinal: that is, it set down rules of belief and behavior. For only one Judaism, the one that made its statement through the Talmud, did (and does) the Torah consist of the laws of life — faithful conviction, right conduct — and also the laws of rational thought. The Bavli in particular lays out the how of the Torah, as well as the what: the rules of thought as well as of life, how God thinks as well as what it means to be "holy, for I the Lord your God am holy."

Thus the Talmud states that only when we understand the how and what of the Torah can we gain access to the will of God for us and the mind of God that formed the will. Rightly read, the Torah teaches not only the various rules that guide but the principles that generate those rules, the premises that link principle to principle, the deep structure of intellect that comes to the surface in those premises, that is, the structure of mind, the integrity of truth, the oneness of the One who is (for that very reason) the one and sole God. That is the power of this Judaism; for a long time, and for the majority of practitioners of Judaism(s) today, this approach defined the normative, the classical, the authentic Torah (i.e., Judaism).

This formulation of the theology of Judaism, which is to say, of the Torah, therefore constitutes the Talmud's representation of the Torah. But such a conception of how to present the Torah, that is, as a statement of humanity's guide to the mind of God, the path to the integrity of truth, did not always characterize the unfolding canon of that very Judaism of the dual Torah that identifies the Talmud as its summa. All prior writings — the Pentateuch (450 B.C.E.); the Mishnah and Tosefta (200

C.E. and afterward); the Talmud of the Land of Israel (i.e., the Yerushalmi), which is the first of the two Talmuds (400); Sifra (to Leviticus); Sifré to Numbers; Sifré to Deuteronomy (all: ca. 250–300); Genesis Rabbah; Leviticus Rabbah; Pesiqta deRab Kahana (ca. 450–500) — present propositions. None of them sets forth propositions through the medium of sustained, dialectical argument. Some (the written Torah, some compositions of aggadic character) appeal to narrative to make their points; some (the Mishnah and the Tosefta) appeal to straightforward demonstration in syllogisms; others still (the Midrash compilations, the Talmud of the Land of Israel) appeal to exegesis of a received text (Scripture, the Mishnah). All of them say in so many words whatever it is that they wish to offer as their statement of the Torah. They make their statement, they spell it out, they clarify it, then they conclude. What makes the second Talmud unique in context is its insistence that to know the Torah, we have to think in the way in which the Torah teaches us to think. And no prior document spells this out in such massive, tedious, repetitive detail, case by case by case, as does the Talmud of Babylonia.

It follows that for the authors of the compositions collected in all of the prior documents and for the compilers of their composites, the Torah comprises the contents of their work, and the purpose of "tradition" is to preserve and hand on propositions. But none of the received documents prior to the Talmud of Babylonia, including the earlier Talmud, shifts the burden of tradition from what God wants alone, as exposed in the Torah, to how God thinks in addition, which also is exposed therein. For the framers of the Bavli, what it means to be "in our image, after our likeness" is to act like God: "You shall be holy as I the Lord your God am holy; just as I am merciful and long-suffering, so must you be merciful and long-suffering"; "You shall be holy, for I the Lord your God am holy." That is to say: "If you sanctify yourselves, I shall credit it to you as though you had sanctified me, and if you do not sanctify yourselves, I shall hold that it is as if you have not sanctified me" (Sifra 195:1.3A–B). To be "in our image" is also to think in full consciousness, in accord with articulated rules of rationality, like God. The Torah teaches how God speaks, therefore how God thinks — but it is only in the Talmud that we find a sustained and articulated effort to show in detail the meaning of that how.

From the time of its closure to the present, this Talmud has served as the summa of Judaism. The Judaic systems that succeeded from then to now have referred back to the Bavli as authoritative; they have formulated their statements in relationship to the Bavli, often in the guise of commentaries or secondary expositions of statements made in it; and they have taken over the Bavli as the backbone for the law and culture that these continuating — and successor — systems proposed to set forth. To establish a truth, appeal to the highest court alone would serve: the court formed by those who have mastered the Bavli, its commentaries, codes, and accompanying responses. Further, until the twentieth century, all Judaisms classified as heretical formed their heresies in response to the Bavli's norms. Therefore, by "classic" we mean authoritative, enduring, and defining; the Bavli is Judaism's classic. Now, since the Bavli is only one among the score or more of large and important documents of classics of the formative age, we have to ask ourselves: Why among all the documents of Judaism did the Bavli gain priority, indeed establish hegemony?

The Bavli is a religious statement of a religious system. An answer to a question about a religious system must appeal to the considerations that govern in the realm of religious truth. Namely, one must ask: Is the system cogent, proportioned, encompassing, and possessed of integrity? Compared with the prior documents of the oral Torah, the Bavli thinks more deeply about deep things, and, in the end, its authors think about different things from those that occupy the earlier writers. Take the Talmud of the Land of Israel, for example. The first Talmud analyzes evidence, the second investigates premises; the first remains wholly within the limits of its case, the second vastly transcends them; the first wants to know the rule, the second asks about the principle and its implications for other cases. The one Talmud provides an exegesis and amplification of the Mishnah, the other, a theoretical study of the law in all its magnificent abstraction — transforming the Mishnah into testimony to a deeper reality altogether, that is, to the law behind the laws.

What characterizes the Bavli and not any prior document seen whole is the sustained and relentless search for the unitary foundations of the diverse laws through an inquiry into the premises of discrete rules, the comparison and contrast of those premises, the statement of the emergent principles, and the comparison and contrast of those principles with the ones that come from other cases and their premises — a process, an inquiry without end into the law behind the laws. What the Bavli wants, beyond its presentation of the positions at hand, is to draw attention to the premises of those positions, the reasoning behind them, the evidence that supports them, the argument that transforms evidence into demonstration, and even the authority, among those who settle questions by expressing opinions, that can hold the combination of principles or premises that underpin a given position.

The real difference between the Bavli and all prior documents of the oral Torah, including the earlier Talmud, emerges from one trait: the Bavli's completely different theory of what it wishes to investigate. And that difference comes from the reason the framers of the Bavli's compositions and composites did the work to begin with. The outlines of the intellectual character of the work flow from the purpose of the project, not the reverse; hence, the modes of thought, the specifics of analytical initiative, are secondary to intellectual morphology. First comes the motivation for thought, then the morphology of thought, then the media of thought.

The difference between prior writings of the oral Torah and the Bavli is the difference between fact and truth, detail and principle, jurisprudence and philosophy; the one kind of writing is a work of exegesis in search of system, the other of analysis in quest of philosophical truth. The Yerushalmi, the first commentary to the Mishnah, for instance, presents the laws, the rule for this, the rule for that, pure and simple; "law" bears its conventional meaning of jurisprudence. The Bavli presents the law in the philosophical sense of the law behind the laws. And that, we see, is not really "law" in any ordinary sense of jurisprudence; it is law in a deeply philosophical sense; it is the rules that govern the way things are, that define what is proportionate, orderly, and properly composed.

The Bavli's framers are uninterested in conclusions and out-come; the deep structure of reason is their goal, and the only way to penetrate into how things are at their foundations is to investigate how conflicting positions rest on principles to be exposed and juxtaposed, balanced, and, if possible, negoti-ated, or, if necessary, left in the balance. The Bavli's authors manage to lay matters out in a very distinctive way. And that way yields as a sustained, somewhat intricate argument (re-quiring us to keep in the balance both names and positions of authorities, and also the objective issues and facts) what the Yerushalmi's method of representation gives as a rather simple sequence of arguments. If we say that the Bavli is "dialectical," presenting a moving argument, from point to point, and the Yerushalmi is static, through such a reductive understatement we should vastly misrepresent the difference. The Bavli's pre-sentation is one of thrust and parry, challenge and response, assertion and counterassertion, theoretical possibility and its exposure to practical facts ("If I had to rely,...I might have supposed..."), and, of course, the authorities of the Bavli are even prepared to rewrite the received Tannaite formulation. This initiative can come only from someone totally in com-mand of the abstractions and able to say that the details have to be precisely this way; so the rule of mind requires; and so it shall be.

The Bavli attained intellectual hegemony over the mind of Israel because its framers set forth their medium in such a way that the implicit message gained immediacy in the heat of ar-gument; so, as a matter of fact, argument about the law served as a mode of serving God through study of the Torah. But its true power derived from the message: that the truth, like God, is one — and the unity makes all the difference. In the Bavli, the written Torah, with its proclamation of the unity and integrity of the one true God, reached its climax in the demonstration of the unity and integrity of truth: God's mind and humanity's mind are one, which is how humanity can, to begin with, know God at all. Now we want to know precisely what it means in Ju-daism to meet God in the Torah, which is to say, to know God the way Judaism maintains we do.

2

How We Meet God in the Torah

Torah Study, Transformation, and Salvation

What happens to us — Israel — in Torah study as portrayed in the Talmud of the Land of Israel and related writings that does not happen to us in any other activity is important for this reason: by Torah study we are changed in our very being, not alone as to knowledge or even as to virtue and taxic status, but as to what we are. Knowledge not only informs; it transforms. Through learning in the Torah we become something different from, better and more holy than, what we were. Through that learning we meet God, God's mind and our mind coming together in shared rationality. How do we know that we have been changed by Torah study? The marks of the transformation emerge in the supernatural power that we have by reason of our (new) knowledge, learning in the Torah.

Torah study produces knowledge that is transitive and transformative; it joins two quite distinct categories: intellect and personal salvation or regeneration. This jarring juxtaposition, identifying ignorance (not knowing a given fact) with the personal condition of unregeneracy, relates what need not, and commonly is not, correlated: the moral or existential condition of the person and the level of intellectual enlightenment of that same person. Knowledge of the Torah, as portrayed in the Talmud and related writings, quite specifically changed a person and made him (never her — until the twentieth century!) simply different from what he had been before or without that same

This chapter was written by Jacob Neusner and revised by Bruce D. Chilton.

50

knowledge: physically weaker, but also strengthened by power that some might call magical but that those who understand it call supernatural.

Before proceeding, let me give a good example of what I mean by knowledge of Torah represented as transformative and salvific. I point to a story that explicitly states the proposition that obeying the Torah, with obedience founded on one's own knowledge of it, constitutes a source of salvation. In this story we shall see that because people observed the rules of the Torah, they expected to be saved. And if they did not observe, they accepted their punishment. So the Torah now stands for something more than revelation and life of study; accordingly, the sage now appears as a holy, not merely a learned, man. This is because his knowledge of the Torah has transformed him. We deal with a category of stories and sayings about the Torah entirely different from what has gone before. We find at Y. Taan. 3:8 one among numerous examples in which the symbol of the Torah and knowledge of the Torah bear salvific consequence, a claim never set forth in the Mishnah in behalf of knowledge, let alone knowledge of the Torah:

II. A. As to Levi ben Sisi: troops came to his town. He took a scroll of the Torah and went up to the roof and said, "Lord of the ages! If a single word of this scroll of the Torah has been nullified [in our town], let them come up against us, and if not, let them go their way."

   B. Forthwith people went looking for the troops but did not find them [because they had gone their way].

   C. A disciple of his did the same thing, and his hand withered, but the troops went their way.

   D. A disciple of his disciple did the same thing. His hand did not wither, but they also did not go their way.

   E. This illustrates the following apophthegm: You can't insult an idiot, and dead skin does not feel the scalpel. (Y. Taan. 3:8)

What is interesting here is how *taxa* into which the word "Torah" previously fell have been absorbed and superseded in a new *taxon*. The Torah is an object: "He took a scroll." It also constitutes God's revelation to Israel: "If a single word . . . " The outcome of the revelation is to form an ongoing way of life, embodied in the sage himself: "A disciple of his did the same thing." The sage plays an intimate part in the supernatural event: "His hand withered." Here the Torah is a source of salvation. How so? The Torah stands for, or constitutes, the way in which the people Israel saves itself from marauders. This straightforward sense of salvation will not have surprised the author of Deuteronomy. But in our documents, there is more in the relationship of the Torah to salvation than mere obedience to its rules.

For now we discern an approach to the learning of the Torah — as distinct from obedience to its rules — that promises not merely intellectual enlightenment but personal renewal, or transfiguration, or some other far-reaching change. In the Yerushalmi and related Midrash compilations we confront a Torah, knowledge of which not merely informs or presents right rules of conduct but which transforms, regenerates, saves. In that context and by these definitions, the theory of the Torah and of Torah study promises a fully realized transformation to those who study and therefore know the Torah. They gain not merely intellectual enlightenment but supernatural power and standing. This power encompassed such salvation as would take place prior to the end of time. The new learning, defined as the consequence of Torah study, changes not merely the mind but the moral and salvific condition of the one who engages in that learning.

This conception would have surprised the prevailing philosophical traditions. In them the consequence of enlightenment in intellect cannot be said to have encompassed personal salvation (let alone national salvation, which the Talmud covers as well). Virtue depended upon right thinking, for example, knowing what is the good, the true, and the beautiful. Knowledge of the Torah had served, for example, the Israelite priesthood as a medium of validation. Through knowledge they knew how to do their job, but it was a job that they got by reason of genealogy, not knowledge. So too, the Israelite scribes identified knowledge of the Torah as the foundation of their professional qualification.

This theory of meeting God in the Torah first came to expression in M. Hag. 2:1, where we see statements about knowledge

possessing traits that are wholly secular; correct knowledge required attention to status (i.e., that of the sage) and to the source
and character of learning (the sage "understands of his own
knowledge," whatever that means):

A. [He] do[es] not expound upon the laws of prohibited relationships [Leviticus 18] before three persons, the works of creation
   [Genesis 13] before two, or the chariot [Ezekiel 1] before one,

B. unless he was a sage and understands of his own knowledge.

C. Whoever reflects upon four things would have been better off
   had he not been born:

D. what is above, what is below, what is before, and what is
   beyond.

E. And whoever has no concern for the glory of his Maker would
   have been better off had he not been born. (M. Hag. 2:1)

These sentences have been quite plausibly interpreted to refer to
personal, not merely intellectual, change effected by knowledge.
But they then do not impute to Torah study as a general classification of intellectual activity the potentiality of (dangerous)
change in one's own being. They speak only of specific topics
and texts. The statements before us identify a very few specific
passages and do not contain the conception that studying the
Torah in general constitutes a transformative and salvific action.

When we come to tractate Abot, a generation beyond the
Mishnah (ca. 250 C.E.), we find heavy emphasis upon the importance of correlating one's actions with one's knowledge. A
variety of sayings insist that if one knows the Torah but does
not act in accord with its teachings, one gains nothing. One
must change one's life to conform with one's knowledge of the
Torah. That point of insistence, of course, invites as its next,
small step, the doctrine that knowing the Torah changes one in
being and essence, not only intellectually, by reason of illumination, but taxically, by reason of transformation. A further step in
the approach to knowledge of the Torah — one that would treat
knowing the Torah on its own as a medium for one's transformation from merely natural to supernatural character — would
be some time in coming and would make its appearance only in
the Yerushalmi and related Midrash compilations. A survey of

tractate Abot yields no such conception, but only the point that knowledge must be confirmed in deeds, a conception of moral but not existential weight, as in the following saying in Abot:

> A. Simeon his son says, "Not the learning is the main thing but the doing. And whoever talks too much causes sin." (Abot 1:17)

True, the statement (see below) that if one keeps his eye on three things, he will not sin, can yield the conception that knowledge bears salvific consequence. But this does not speak of a personal transformation in one's status and condition. The knowledge that saves us from sin is instrumental, not transformative:

> Know what is above you: (1) An eye which sees, and (2) an ear which hears, and (3) all your actions are written down in a book. (Abot 3:1)

The same conception, that knowledge is essential to attitudes that bring salvation, is stated in the following:

> A. Aqabiah b. Mehallalel says, "Reflect upon three things and you will not fall into the clutches of transgression:
>
> B. "Know (1) from whence you come, (2) whither you are going, and (3) before whom you are going to have to give a full account [of yourself].
>
> C. "From whence do you come? From a putrid drop.
>
> D. "Whither are you going? To a place of dust, worms, and maggots.
>
> E. "And before whom are you going to give a full account of yourself? Before the King of kings of kings, the Holy One, blessed be he." (Abot 3:1)

We have not strayed far from the notion that knowledge of the Torah promises a good reward here and after death because it keeps us from sin, that is to say, the position, vis-à-vis studying a trade, of *Nehorai*. Here again, knowledge is treated in an instrumental sense; it yields a given goal; it does not effect a desired transformation. A promise that in context is quite consistent is that if I study the Torah, I encounter God:

> C. R. Hananiah b. Teradion says, "[If] two sit together and between them do not pass teachings of Torah, lo, this is a seat of the scornful....

E. "Two who are sitting, and words of Torah do pass between them — the Presence is with them, as it is said, 'Then they that feared the Lord spoke with one another, and the Lord hearkened and heard, and a book of remembrance was written before him, for them that feared the Lord and gave thought to his name' (Mal. 3:16)....

G. "I know that this applies to two.

H. "How do I know that even if a single person sits and works on Torah, the Holy One, blessed be he, sets aside a reward for him? As it is said, 'Let him sit alone and keep silent, because he has laid it upon him' " (Lam. 3:28). (Abot 3:2)

A. R. Halafta of Kefar Hananiah says, "Among ten who sit and work hard on Torah the Presence comes to rest,

B. "as it is said, 'God stands in the congregation of God' (Ps. 82:1).

C. "And how do we know that the same is so even of five? For it is said, 'And he has founded his group upon the earth' (Amos 9:6).

D. "And how do we know that this is so even of three? Since it is said, 'And he judges among the judges' (Ps. 82:1).

E. "And how do we know that this is so even of two? Because it is said, 'Then they that feared the Lord spoke with one another, and the Lord hearkened and heard' (Mal. 3:16).

F. "And how do we know that this is so even of one? Since it is said, 'In every place where I record my name I will come to you and I will bless you' " (Exod. 20:24). (Abot 3:6)

"Knowing God" or bringing God into one's study circle certainly represents desirable goals of illumination. But these do not encompass the transformative experience promised later on in the Talmud to the one who knows. Why not? Because even though God has joined my study circle and brought the divine presence to rest among the disciples, we still do not then claim supernatural powers as the consequence.

The contrast between getting a good name for oneself and "getting" the teachings of the Torah, as in the following saying, also is not quite to the point:

[If] one has gotten a good name, he has gotten it for himself.
[If] he has gotten teachings of Torah, he has gotten himself life
eternal.

Here we speak of repute, a form of virtue, but not wonder working. Moreover, the same point as Simeon's, above, comes to the
fore in the following:

A. R. Haninah b. Dosa says, "For anyone whose fear of sin takes
   precedence over his wisdom, his wisdom will endure.

B. "And for anyone whose wisdom takes precedence over his fear
   of sin, his wisdom will not endure."

C. He would say, "Anyone whose deeds are more than his
   wisdom — his wisdom will endure.

D. "And anyone whose wisdom is more than his deeds — his
   wisdom will not endure." (Abot 3:9)

 I. He would say, "Anyone whose wisdom is greater than his
    deeds — to what is he to be likened? To a tree with abundant
    foliage, but few roots.

 J. "When the winds come, they will uproot it and blow it down.

K. "As it is said, 'He shall be like a tamarisk in the desert and
   shall not see when good comes but shall inhabit the parched
   places in the wilderness' (Jer. 17:6).

L. "But anyone whose deeds are greater than his wisdom — to
   what is he to be likened? To a tree with little foliage but
   abundant roots.

M. "For even if all the winds in the world were to come and blast
   at it, they will not move it from its place.

N. "As it is said, 'He shall be as a tree planted by the waters, and
   that spreads out its roots by the river, and shall not fear when
   heat comes, and his leaf shall be green, and shall not be careful
   in the year of drought, neither shall cease from yielding fruit'
   (Jer. 17:8)." (Abot 3:17)

A. R. Ishmael, his son, says, "He who learns so as to teach — they
   give him a chance to learn and to teach.

B. "He who learns so as to carry out his teachings — they give
   him a chance to learn, to teach, to keep, and to do." (Abot 4:5)

A variety of sayings, indeed, explicitly identify not Torah learn-ing but other virtues as primary, and furthermore scarcely concede to Torah learning transformative, let alone salvific, power:

> C. R. Simeon says, "There are three crowns: the crown of Torah, the crown of priesthood, and the crown of sovereignty.
>
> D. "But the crown of a good name is best of them all." (Abot 4:13)

> A. He would say, "Better is a single moment spent in penitence and good deeds in this world than the whole of the world to come.
>
> B. "And better is a single moment of inner peace in the world to come than the whole of a lifetime spent in this world." (Abot 4:17)

These and similar sayings attest to a variety of modes of human regeneration, none of them connected with Torah learning in particular.

Now, as a matter of fact, in the two Talmuds and related Midrash compilations, a quite different theory of Torah learning predominates. It is simply the fact that knowledge of the Torah changes the one who knows. He becomes physically weaker but gains, in compensation, supernatural powers. The legitimating power of the Torah and its study found in the pages of the Tal-mud of the Land of Israel is explicit: knowledge of the Torah changes a man into a sage and also saves Israel. The Torah then involves not mere knowledge, for example, correct information or valid generalization, but saving knowledge.

One important qualification is required. Knowledge is not the only medium of salvation. Salvation, as before, comes from keeping the law of the Torah. Keeping the law in the right way is the way to bring the Messiah, the son of David. This is stated by Levi, as follows: "If Israel would keep a single Sab-bath in the proper way, forthwith the son of David would come" (Y. Taan. 1:1.9). But the issue of not doing but (mere) knowing, of salvation through study of the Torah, is distinct.

Torah Study and Supernatural Power

To the rabbis the principal salvific deed was to "study Torah," by which they meant memorizing Torah sayings by constant repetition and, as the Talmud itself amply testifies, for some sages profound analytic inquiry into the meaning of those sayings. This act of "study of Torah" imparted supernatural power. For example, by repeating words of Torah, the sage could ward off the angel of death and accomplish other kinds of miracles as well. So Torah formulas served as incantations. Mastery of Torah transformed the man who engaged in Torah learning into a supernatural figure, able to do things ordinary folk could not do. In the nature of things, the category of "Torah" was vastly expanded so that the symbol of Torah, a Torah scroll, could be compared to a man of Torah, namely, a rabbi. Since what made a man into a sage or a disciple of a sage or a rabbi was studying the Torah through discipleship, what is at stake in the symbolic transfer is quite obvious.

The Torah is, then, identified with and personified by the sage; so he is changed because of what he knows. This is a material and palpable claim, not a mere mode of ascription of great sanctity, lacking any concrete consequence. And this is a vastly expanded definition of the symbol of "Torah." The claim that a sage (or disciple of a sage) himself was equivalent to a scroll of the Torah forms a material, legal comparison, not merely a symbolic metaphor:

> A. He who sees a disciple of a sage who has died is as if he sees a scroll of the Torah that has been burned. (Y. Moed Qat. 3:7.10)

> I. R. Jacob bar Abayye in the name of R. Aha: "An elder who forgot his learning because of some accident which happened to him — they treat him with the sanctity owed to an ark [of the Torah]." (Y. Moed Qat. 3:1.11)

In both instances actual behavior was affected. This view is expressed in stories indicating the belief that while a sage is repeating Torah sayings, the angel of death cannot approach him:

> F. [Proving that while one is studying Torah, the angel of death cannot touch a person, the following is told:] A disciple of

R. Hisda fell sick. He sent two disciples to him, so that they
would repeat Mishnah traditions with him. [The angel of
death] turned himself before them into the figure of a snake,
and they stopped repeating traditions, and [the sick man] died.

G. A disciple of Bar Pedaiah fell ill. He sent to him two disciples to repeat Mishnah traditions with him. [The angel of
death] turned himself before them into a kind of star, and they
stopped repeating Mishnah traditions, and he died. (Y. Moed
Qat. 3:5.21)

Repeating Mishnah traditions thus warded off death. It is
hardly surprising that stories were told about wonders associated with the deaths of various rabbis. These validated the
claim of supernatural power imputed to the rabbis. A repertoire
of such stories includes two sorts.

First, there is a list of supernatural occurrences accompanying sages' deaths, and, second, these make a claim of specific
miracles that were done by heaven when a great sage died. The
former are as in the following:

A. When R. Aha died, a star appeared at noon.

B. When R. Hanah died, the statues bowed down.

C. When R. Yohanan died, the icons bowed down.

D. They said that [this was to indicate] there were no icons like
him [so beautiful as Yohanan himself].

E. When R. Hanina of Bet Hauran died, the Sea of Tiberias
split open.

F. They said that [this was to commemorate the miracle that took
place] when he went up to intercalate the year, and the sea split
open before him.

G. When R. Hoshaiah died, the palm of Tiberias fell down.

H. When R. Isaac b. Elisheb died, seventy [infirm] thresholds of
houses in Galilee were shaken down.

I. They said that [this was to commemorate the fact that] they
[were shaky and] had depended on his merit [for the miracle
that permitted them to continue to stand].

J. When R. Samuel bar R. Isaac died, cedars of the Land of Israel
were uprooted.

K. They said that [this was to take note of the fact that] he would take branch [of a cedar] and [dance, so] praising a bride [at her wedding, and thereby giving her happiness].

L. The rabbis would ridicule them [for lowering himself by doing so]. Said to them R. Zeira, "Leave him be. Does the old man not know what he is doing?"

M. When he died, a flame came forth from heaven and intervened between his bier and the congregation. For three hours there were voices and thunderings in the world: "Come and see what a sprig of cedar has done for this old man!"

N. [Further] an echo came forth and said, "Woe that R. Samuel bar R. Isaac has died, the doer of merciful deeds."

O. When R. Yosa bar Halputa died, the gutters ran with blood in Laodicea.

P. They said [that the reason was] that he had given his life for the rite of circumcision.

Q. When R. Abbahu died, the pillars of Caesarea wept.

R. The [Gentiles] said [that the reason was] that [the pillars] were celebrating. The Israelites said to them, "And do those who are distant [such as yourselves] know why those who are near [we ourselves] are raising a cry?" (Y. Abod. Zar. 3:1.2)

BB. One of the members of the patriarchate died, and the [burial] cave folded over [and received the bier], so endangering the lives [of those who had come to bury him]. R. Yose went up and took leave [of the deceased], saying "Happy is a man who has left this world in peace."

CC. When R. Yosa died, the castle of Tiberias collapsed, and members of the patriarchate were rejoicing. R. Zeira said to them, "There is no similarity [between this case and the miracle described at BB]. The peoples' lives were endangered, here no one's life was endangered. In that case, no pagan worship was removed, while here, an idol was uprooted [so, consequently, the event described in BB was not a miracle, while the event described here was a miracle and a sign of divine favor]." (Y. Abod. Zar. 3:1.2)

What is important in the foregoing anthology is the linkage between the holy deeds of the sage and the miracles done at his demise. The sages' merit, attained through study of Torah or through acts of saintliness and humility, was demonstrated for all to see. So the sage was not merely a master of Torah. But his mastery of Torah laid the foundations for all the other things he was: he was changed into something other than what he had been before he studied the Torah, and all else follows.

The second type of story — which tells of specific miracles as distinct from natural wonders — was related with regard to the death of the patriarch:

E. R. Nathan in the name of R. Mana: "There were miracles done that day. It was the eve of the Sabbath, and all the villagers assembled to make a lamentation for him. They put down the bier eighteen times en route to burial to mourn him, and they accompanied him down to Bet Shearim. The daylight was protracted until each one of them had reached his home [in time for the Sabbath] and had time to fill up a jug of water and light the Sabbath lamp. When the sun set, the cock crowed, and the people began to be troubled, saying, 'Perhaps we have violated the Sabbath.'

F. "But an echo came to them, 'Whoever did not refrain from participation in the lamentations for Rabbi may be given the good news that he is going to enjoy a portion in the world to come,

G. " 'except for the launderer [who used to come to Rabbi day by day, but did not bother to participate in his funeral].' When he heard this, he went up to the roof and threw himself down and died. Then an echo went forth and said, 'Even the laundryman [will enjoy the life of the world to come].' " (Y. Ket. 12:3.4)

J. When R. Huna, the exilarch, died, they brought his bones up here. They said, "If we are going to bury him properly, let us place him near R. Hiyya, because he comes from there."

K. They said, "Who is worthy of placing him there?"

L. Said to them R. Haggai, "I shall go up and place him there."

M. They said to him, "You are looking for an excuse, for you are an old man, so you want to go up there and die and be buried there next to Hiyya."

N. He said to them, "Tie a rope to my feet, and if I delay there too long you can drag me out."

O. He went in and found three biers.

P. [He heard,] "Judah, my son, is after you, and no one else. Hezekiah, my son, is after you, and no one else. Joseph, son of Israel, and no one else."

Q. He raised his eyes and looked. One said to him, "Lower your face."

R. Said R. Hiyya the Elder, "Judah, my son, make room for R. Huna."

S. He made a place for him, but [Huna] did not accept being buried [next to Hiyya the Elder, out of modesty].

T. [Haggai] said, "Just as [out of modesty] he did not accept being buried next to him, so may his seed never die out."

U. R. Haggai left that place at the age of eighty years, and they doubled the number of his years [so that he lived another eighty years]. (Y. Ketub. 12:3.7)

That the sage was different from ordinary men seems to be well established. But in context that claim was not surprising; holy men in general were deemed supernatural. What makes this claim distinctive in the present system is not only that it is unprecedented in its canonical context but also that it is a claim of supernatural power gained specifically through the act of undertaking to study the Torah.

The Torah, of course, was deemed true, and that explained why rabbis were shown as more effective than other magicians, specifically in those very same settings where, all parties conceded, other wonder workers, as much as rabbis, were able to perform magical deeds. What is important in the following is the fact that in a direct contest between a rabbi and another sort of magician, an Israelite heretic, the rabbi was shown to enjoy superior magical power:

A. When R. Eleazar, R. Joshua, and R. Aqiba went in to bathe in the baths of Tiberias, a *min* [in context: Israelite heretic] saw them. He said what he said, and the arched chamber in the bath [where idolatrous statues were put up] held them fast [so that they could not move].

B. Said R. Eleazar to R. Joshua, "Now Joshua b. Hananiah, see what you can do."

C. When that *min* tried to leave, R. Joshua said what he said, and the doorway of the bath seized and held the *min* firm, so that whoever went in had to give him a knock [to push by], and whoever went out had to give him a knock [to push by].

D. He said to them, "Undo whatever you have done [to let me go]."

E. They said to him, "Release us, and we shall release you."

F. They released one another.

G. Once they got outside, said R. Joshua to that *min*, "Lo, you have learned [from us whatever you are going to learn]."

H. He said, "Let's go down to the sea."

I. When they got down to the sea, that *min* said whatever it was that he said, and the sea split open.

J. He said to them, "Now is this not what Moses, your rabbi, did at the sea?"

K. They said to him, "Do you not concede to us that Moses, our rabbi, walked through it?"

L. He said to them, "Yes."

M. They said to him, "Then walk through it."

N. He walked through it.

O. R. Joshua instructed the ruler of the sea, who swallowed him up.

IV. A. When R. Eliezer, R. Joshua, and Rabban Gamaliel went up to Rome, they came to a certain place and found children making little piles [of dirt]. They said, "Children of the Land of Israel make this sort of thing, and they say, 'This is heave offering,' and 'That is tithe.' It's likely that there are Jews here."

B. They came into one place and were received there.

C. When they sat down to eat, [they noticed] that each dish which they brought into them would first be brought into a small room, and then would be brought to them, and they wondered whether they might be eating sacrifices offered to the dead. [That is, before the food was brought to them, it was brought into a small chamber, in which, they suspected, sacrifices were taken from each dish and offered to an idol.]

D. They said to [the host], "What is your purpose, in the fact that, as to every dish which you bring before us, if you do not bring it first into a small room, you do not bring it in to us?"

E. He said to them, "I have a very old father, and he has made a decree for himself that he will never go out of that small room until he will see the sages of Israel."

F. They said to him, "Go and tell him, 'Come out here to them, for they are here.'"

G. He came out to them.

H. They said to him, "Why do you do this?"

I. He said to them, "Pray for my son, for he has not produced a child."

J. Said R. Eliezer to R. Joshua, "Now, Joshua b. Hananiah, let us see what you will do."

K. He said to them, "Bring me flax seeds," and they brought him flax seeds.

L. He appeared to sow the seed on the table; he appeared to scatter the seed; he appeared to bring the seed up; he appeared to take hold of it, until he drew up a woman, holding on to her tresses.

M. He said to her, "Release whatever [magic] you have done [to this man]."

N. She said to him, "I am not going to release [my spell]."

O. He said to her, "If you don't do it, I shall publicize your [magical secrets]."

P. She said to him, "I cannot do it, for [the magical materials] have been cast into the sea."

Q. R. Joshua made a decree that the sea release [the magical materials], and they came up.

R. They prayed for [the host], and he had the merit of begetting a son, R. Judah b. Bathera.

S. They said, "If we came up here only for the purpose of begetting that righteous man, it would have been enough for us."

T. Said R. Joshua b. Hananiah, "I can take cucumbers and pump-
kins and turn them into rams and hosts of rams, and they will
produce still more." (Y. Sanh. 7:12.3)

These extracts leave no doubt that the Talmud imputed to
Israel's sages precisely the powers generally assigned to magicians. The sage did exactly what the magician did, only he
did it better. When the magician then pretended to do what
Moses had done, it was his end. The story about Joshua's magic
in Rome is similar; it makes explicit reference to sympathetic
magic (K–L). The result was the discovery that the childless
man had been subject to a spell. There can be no doubt that distinctions between magic and supernatural power meant nothing
to the Talmud's storytellers. The clerks were not merely holy
men; they were a particular kind of holy men. In consequence
of the belief that rabbis had magical powers, it was quite natural
to impute to rabbis the ability both to bless those who favored
them and to curse those who did not.

The Sage and the Formation of Torah

Thus far I have shown only that sages studied the Torah and
that through that study they gained supernatural standing (e.g.,
when they were buried) and power, which they attributed to
their knowledge of the Torah. What I have yet to demonstrate
is that knowledge of the Torah itself changed the sage in such
a way that he could manipulate the supernatural power inher-
ing in the Torah, and also could himself join in the processes
of forming the Torah. I have alleged that the man himself
was transformed through Torah study. And what I have already offered in evidence demands an explanation of how that
transformation took place. For the allegation that knowledge in
particular changes the person can itself refer to a merely instrumental power: if I know thus and so, I can do such and such.
At stake in the Yerushalmi's theory of the Torah was a much
different power.

Specifically, if a man knows the Torah, he can join in the making of the Torah, and that claim in his behalf as a sage forms
solid evidence of the allegation that studying the Torah not only

endows him with power but actually changes him from what he had been into something else. He had been ordinary; now he is not merely powerful but holy. And his holiness is shown by the fact that, just as he studies the Torah in its written and oral forms, so he may study the Torah in its everyday form: the sage himself, his gestures, his actions then forming precedents valid within the practice of the Torah itself. And when I allege that because we have studied the Torah, we are changed, so that we can now join in the process of revealing the Torah, I am likewise alleging that studying the Torah provides an experience of transformation, regeneration, and salvation. Accordingly, I have now to demonstrate that the supernatural status accorded to the person of the sage endowed his deeds with normative, therefore revelatory, power.

What the sage did had the status of law; the sage was the model of the law, thus having been changed, transformed, regenerated, saved, turned by studying the Torah into the human embodiment of the Torah. This view of Torah study as transformative and salvific — now without explicit appeal to deeds in conformity to the law, though surely that is taken for granted — accounts for the position that the sage was a holy man. For what made the sage distinctive was his combination of this-worldly authority and power and otherworldly influence. In the Yerushalmi's view, the clerk in the court and the holy man on the rooftop praying for rain, or calling heaven to defend the city against marauders, were one and the same. The tight union between salvation and law, the magical power of the sage and his lawgiving authority, was effected through the integrative act of studying the Torah. And that power of integration accounts for the successor-system's insistence that if the sage exercised supernatural power as a kind of living Torah, his very deeds served to reveal law, as much as his word expressed revelation.

The capacity of the sage to participate in the process of revelation is illustrated in two types of materials. First, tales told about rabbis' behavior on specific occasions immediately are translated into rules for the entire community to keep. Accordingly, the rabbi was a source not merely of good example but of prescriptive law. Here is a humble and mundane case of how that view came to expression:

X. R. Aha went to Emmaus, and he ate dumpling [prepared by Samaritans].

Y. R. Jeremiah ate leavened bread prepared by them.

Z. R. Hezekiah ate their locusts prepared by them.

AA. R. Abbahu prohibited Israelite use of wine prepared by them. (Y. Abod. Zar. 5:4.3)

These reports of what rabbis had done enjoyed the same authority as statements of the law on eating what Samaritans cooked, as did citations of traditions in the names of the great authorities of old or of the day. If a person was a sage of sufficient standing, what he did served as a norm.

Far more common in the Talmud are instances of the second type of material — tales in which the deed of a rabbi is adduced as an authoritative precedent for the law under discussion. It was everywhere taken for granted that what a rabbi did, he did because of his mastery of the law. Even though a formulation of the law was not in hand, a tale about what a rabbi actually did constituted adequate evidence on how to formulate the law itself. So from the practice of an authority, a law might be framed quite independently of the person of the sage. The sage then functioned as a lawgiver, like Moses. Among a great many instances of that mode of generating law are the following:

A. Gamaliel Zuga was walking along, leaning on the shoulder of R. Simeon b. Laqish. They came across an image.

B. He said to him, "What is the law as to passing before it?"

C. He said to him, "Pass before it, but close [your] eyes."

D. R. Isaac was walking along, leaning on the shoulder of R. Yohanan. They came across an idol before the council building.

E. He said to him, "What is the law as to passing before it?"

F. He said to him, "Pass before it, but close [your] eyes."

G. R. Jacob bar Idi was walking along, leaning upon R. Joshua b. Levi. They came across a procession in which an idol was carried. He said to him, "Nahum, the most holy man, passed before this idol, and will you not pass by it? Pass before it but close your eyes." (Y. Abod. Zar. 3:11.2)

FF. R. Aha had chills and fever. [They brought him] a medicinal drink prepared from the phallus of Dionysian revelers. But he would not drink it. They brought it to R. Jonah, and he did drink it. Said R. Mana, "Now if R. Jonah, the patriarch, had known what it was, he would never have drunk it."

GG. Said R. Huna, "That is to say, 'They do not accept healing from something that derives from an act of fornication.'" (Y. Abod. Zar. 2:2.3)

What is important is GG, the restatement of the story in the form of a fixed rule, hence as a law. The example of a rabbi served to teach how one should live a truly holy life. The requirements went far beyond the measure of the law; they extended to refraining from deeds of a most commonplace sort. Moreover, the example of rabbinical virtue was adduced explicitly to account for the supernatural or magical power of a rabbi. There was no doubt in people's imagination, therefore, that the reason rabbis could do the amazing things people said they did was that they embodied the law and exercised its supernatural or magical power. The correlation between learning and teaching, on the one side, and supernatural power or recognition, on the other, is explicit in the following:

A. R. Yosa fasted eighty fasts in order to see R. Hiyya the Elder [in a dream]. He finally saw him, and his hands trembled and his eyes grew dim.

B. Now if you say that R. Yosa was an unimportant man, [and so was unworthy of such a vision, that is not the case]. For a weaver came before R. Yohanan. He said to him, "I saw in my dream that the heaven fell, and one of your disciples was holding it up."

C. He said to him, "Will you know him [when you see him]?"

D. He said to him, "When I see him, I shall know him." Then all of his disciples passed before him, and he recognized R. Yosa.

E. R. Simeon b. Laqish fasted three hundred fasts in order to have a vision of R. Hiyya the Elder, but he did not see him.

F. Finally he began to be distressed about the matter. He said, "Did he labor in learning of Torah more than I?"

G. They said to him, "He brought Torah to the people of Israel to a greater extent than you have, and not only so, but he even went into exile [to teach on a wider front]."

H. He said to them, "And did I not go into exile too?"

I. They said to him, "You went into exile only to learn, but he went into exile to teach others." (Y. Ketub. 12:3.7)

This story shows that the storyteller regarded as a fact of life the correlation between mastery of Torah sayings and supernatural power — visions of the deceased, in this case. This is why Simeon b. Laqish complained (E–F) that he had learned as much Torah as the other and so had every right to be able to conjure the dead. The greater supernatural power of the other then was explained in terms of the latter's superior service to "Torah." The upshot is that the sage was changed by Torah learning and could save Israel through Torah.

Precisely how did sages explain the transformation effected by study of the Torah? It was by appeal to the character of the saints of Scripture. Seeing Scripture as their own model, they took the position that the Torah of old, its supernatural power and salvific promise, in their own day continued to endure among themselves. By studying the Torah, they turned themselves into models of those sages whose holy deeds the Torah recorded: Moses, David, and Isaiah being called rabbis, for instance. In consequence, the promise of salvation contained in every line of Scripture was to be kept in every deed of learning and obedience to the law effected under their auspices. Learning in the Torah was salvific because it turned ordinary men into saints in the model of the saints of the Torah.

That fact helps us to understand the constant citation of Scripture in the context of sages' rulings and doings. It was not to establish authority alone. Rather, it was also to identify what was happening just then with what had happened long ago. The purpose was not merely to demonstrate and authenticate the bona fide character of a new figure of salvation but also to show the continuity of the salvific process, a process, therefore, that relied for its persistence upon learning in particular. The act of study of the Torah, in the system before us, had to be endowed with supernatural status and supernatural power to save because the act of learning formed the medium for the transmission of not merely the lessons but the supernatural power of old. The Torah presented not merely rules but examples of holiness, and salvation lay in sanctification: "Today, if you repent" (that is, conform now, as not before), you can accept transformation, regeneration, salvation.

It followed that the pattern and promise of salvation contained therein lay within the sages' way of life: studying the Torah in discipleship. That is the meaning of the explicit reading of the present into the past — the implicit arrogation of the hope of the past to the salvific heroes of the present: themselves. To state matters simply, if David, king of Israel, was like a rabbi today, then a rabbi today would be the figure of the son of David who was to come as king of Israel. It is not surprising, therefore, that among the many biblical heroes whom the talmudic rabbis treated as sages, principal and foremost was David himself, now made into a messianic rabbi or a rabbinical Messiah. He was the sage of the Torah, the avatar and model for the sages of their own time. This view was made explicit both specifically and in general terms. If a rabbi was jealous to have his traditions cited in his own name, it was because that was David's explicit view as well.

In more general terms, both David and Moses are represented as students of Torah, just like the disciples and sages of the current time. David is represented as a devoted student of the Torah. Here is one representation of a biblical story in the mode of an academic tale:

A. It is written, "And David said longingly, 'O that someone would give me water to drink from the well of Bethlehem [which is by the gate]' " (1 Chron. 11:17).

B. R. Hiyya bar Ba said, "He required a teaching of law."

C. "Then the three mighty men broke through [the camp of the Philistines]" (1 Chron. 11:18).

D. Why three? Because the law is not decisively laid down by fewer than three.

E. "But David would not drink of it; [he poured it out to the Lord, and said, 'Far be it from me before my God that I should do this. Shall I drink the lifeblood of these men? For at the risk of their lives they brought it']" (1 Chron. 11:18–19).

F. David did not want the law to be laid down in his own name.

G. "He poured it out to the Lord" — establishing [the decision] as [an unattributed] teaching for the generations [so that the law should be authoritative and so be cited anonymously]. (Y. Sanh. 2:6.4)

O. David himself prayed for mercy for himself, as it is said, "Let me dwell in thy tent forever! Oh to be safe under the shelter of thy wings, *selah*" (Ps. 61:4).

P. And did it enter David's mind that he would live forever?

Q. But this is what David said before the Holy One, blessed be he, "Lord of the world, may I have the merit that my words will be stated in synagogues and schoolhouses."

R. Simeon b. Nazira in the name of R. Isaac said, "Every disciple in whose name people cite a teaching of law in this world — his lips murmur with him in the grave, as it is said, 'Your kisses are like the best wine that goes down smoothly, gliding over lips of those that sleep' (Song 7:9).

S. "Just as in the case of a mass of grapes, once a person puts his finger in it, forthwith even his lips begin to smack, so the lips of the righteous, when someone cites a teaching of law in their names — their lips murmur with them in the grave." (Y. Sheqal. 2:4.5)

David as a model of the disciple of the sage is represented in the following for the virtue of conscious and zealous Torah study:

O. "I will awake the dawn" (Ps. 5:7, 8) — I will awaken the dawn; the dawn will not awaken me.

P. David's [evil] impulse tried to seduce him [to sin]. And it would say to him, "David. It is the custom of kings that awakens them. And you say, I will awake the dawn. It is the custom of kings that they sleep until the third hour [of the day]. And you say, At midnight I rise." And [David] used to say [in reply], "[I rise early] because of thy righteous ordinances" (Ps. 119:62).

Q. And what would David do? R. Phineas in the name of R. Eleazar b. R. Menahem [said], "[He used to take a harp and lyre

and set them at his bedside. And he would rise at midnight
and play them so that the associates of Torah should hear. And
what would the associates of Torah say? 'If David involves himself with Torah, how much more so should we.' We find that all
of Israel was involved in Torah [study] on account of David."
(Y. Ber. 1:1.12, trans. Tzvee Zahavy)

This extract shows us how the Talmud's authorities readily saw
their concerns in biblical statements attributed to David. "Water" meant "a teaching of Torah." "Three mighty men" were of
course judges. At issue was whether or not the decision was
to be stated in David's own name — and so removed from the
authoritative consensus of sages. David exhibits precisely those
concerns for the preservation of his views in his name that, in
earlier sections, we saw attributed to rabbis. All of this, as we
have noted, fully reveals the rabbis' deeper convictions when
we remember that David the rabbi was also in everyone's mind
David the Messiah.

Torah Study and *Zekhut*

Enough has been set forth to suggest that I mean to represent
the supernatural theory of the transformation effected by the
study of the Torah as the centerpiece of the Yerushalmi and
related Midrash compilations. But our evidence suggests precisely the opposite. For instance, in stories in the Talmud of the
Land of Israel, knowledge of the Torah is only a step toward a
higher aim: *zekhut* (the heritage of virtue and its consequent entitlements). Futhermore, in the Yerushalmi and related Midrash
compilations, points of integration, not of differentiation, guide
us to the systemic problematic, and thus we must take seriously
the contingent status, the standing of a dependent variable,
accorded to Torah study in such stories as the following:

C. There was a house that was about to collapse over there [in
   Babylonia], and Rab set one of his disciples in the house, until they had cleared out everything from the house. When the
   disciple left the house, the house collapsed.

D. And there are those who say that it was R. Adda bar Ahwah.

E. Sages sent and said to him, "What sort of good deeds are to your credit [that you have that much merit]?"

F. He said to them, "In my whole life no man ever got to the synagogue in the morning before I did. I never left anybody there when I went out. I never walked four cubits without speaking words of Torah. Nor did I ever mention teachings of Torah in an inappropriate setting. I never laid out a bed and slept for a regular period of time. I never took great strides among the associates. I never called my fellow by a nickname. I never rejoiced in the embarrassment of my fellow. I never cursed my fellow when I was lying by myself in bed. I never walked over in the marketplace to someone who owed me money.

G. "In my entire life I never lost my temper in my household."

H. This was meant to carry out that which is stated as follows: "I will give heed to the way that is blameless. Oh when wilt thou come to me? I will walk with integrity of heart within my house" (Ps. 101:2). (Y. Taan. 3:11.4)

What I find striking in this story is that mastery of the Torah is only one means of attaining the *zekhut* that had enabled the sage to keep the house from collapsing. And Torah study is not the primary means of attaining *zekhut*. The question at E provides the key, together with its answer at F. For what the sage did to gain such remarkable *zekhut* is not to master such-and-so many tractates of the Mishnah. It was rather acts of courtesy, consideration, gentility, restraint.

These produced *zekhut*, all of them acts of self-abnegation or the avoidance of power over others, the submission to the will and the requirement of self-esteem of others. Torah study is simply an item on a list of actions or attitudes that generate *zekhut*. Here, in a moral setting, we find the politics replicated: the form of power that the system promises comes from the rejection of power that the world recognizes — legitimate violence replaced by legitimation of the absence of the power to commit violence, or of the failure to commit violence. And when we ask, Whence that sort of power? the answer lies in the gaining of *zekhut* in a variety of ways, not in the acquisition of *zekhut* through the study of the Torah solely or even primarily. But, we note, the story at hand speaks of a sage in particular. He has gained *zekhut* by not acting the way sages are commonly assumed to behave but in a humble way.

In the context of this story, *zekhut* then may prove a virtue dependent upon the situation of the Torah and its study; consequently we should have to impute a systemic priority, indeed a centrality, to the supernatural theory of the value of study of the Torah, finding in the new learning the key to the Yerushalmi and related Midrash compilations as a whole. But this is, in fact, not so. At hand is not a religious system in which the transformation of the individual through salvific knowledge provides the compelling answer to the question of personal salvation. A different question stands at center stage, and a different answer altogether defines the dramatic tension of the theatrical globe. At stake, as we shall now see, is a public and a national question, one concerning Israel's history and destiny, to which the individual and his salvation, while important, are distinctly subordinated. Not Torah study, which may generate *zekhut*, but *zekhut* itself defines what is at issue, namely, the generative problematic of the system; and only when we grasp the answer provided by *zekhut* shall we reach a definition of the question that precipitated the systemic construction and the formation of its categories, principal and contingent alike.

The importance of the transformative theory of the study of the Torah in no way diminishes when we recognize the subordinate position of the Torah in the Yerushalmi and related Midrash compilations. In unifying the distinct categories of learning (rather than deeds or virtue) and one's personal condition in the supernatural world; in recasting the category of worldview from an intellectual and even a moral to a salvific and a supernatural indicator; in encompassing data not formerly noted or even assembled at all — in all these the successor-system's novel power of integration is displayed. If Torah study changes us not only in our knowledge or even virtue but in our relationship to heaven, endowing us with supernatural power, then the system as a whole signals a union of heaven and earth that was formerly unimagined. What we know concerns not only earth but heaven, and the power that knowledge brings governs in both realms.

Study of the Torah changed the one who studied because through it he entered into the mind of God, learning how God's mind worked when God formed the Torah, written and oral alike, and (in the explicit view of Gen. Rab. 1:1) consulted the Torah in creating the world. And there, in the intellect of God, humanity gained access to the only means of uniting intellect with existential condition. The Mishnah had set forth the rules that governed the natural world in relationship to heaven. But knowledge of the Torah now joined the one world, known through nature, with the other world, the world of supernature, where, in the end, intellect merely served in the quest for salvation. Through Torah study sages claimed for themselves a place in that very process of thought that had given birth to nature; but it was a supernatural process, and knowledge of that process on its own terms would transform and, in the nature of things, save. In the end, however, Torah proves contingent and instrumental. Knowing God involves something other than mere mastery of learning and tradition. As we have already noted, there is something more important than Torah study. Let us now turn to *zekhut,* a quite different way of knowing God.

3

How We Know God
in Heart and Soul

Zekhut as Transcending Torah Study

The picture set forth in chapter 2 placed knowledge of the Torah at the center of Judaism. While people suppose that the Torah forms the symbolic center of Judaism, and the study of the Torah the critical action, so that women, excluded from academies, find no place in Judaism at all, in fact when we reach the systemic center, we find that "the study of Torah" does not outweigh all else, not at all. As noted above, stories contained in the Talmud of the Land of Israel — in which the priority and sanctity of the sage's knowledge of the Torah form the focus of discourse — treat study of the Torah as contingent and merely instrumental. Time and again, knowledge of the Torah forms a way-station on a path to a more distant, more central goal: attaining *zekhut*.

Torah study is one means of attaining access to that heritage, of gaining *zekhut*. There are other equally suitable means; furthermore, the merit gained by Torah study is no different from the merit gained by any and all other types of acts of supererogatory grace. And still more astonishing, a single remarkable action may produce *zekhut* of the same order as a lifetime of devotion to Torah study, and a simple ass-driver through a noteworthy act of selfless behavior may attain the same level of *zekhut* as a learned sage.

Were such stories as these located other than in the Talmud, one might be tempted by the thesis that they represented

an antirabbinic viewpoint. But rabbis told these stories, preserved them, and placed them on exhibition to expose the finest
virtue they could imagine. This is why we turn for our integrat-
ing conception to that final reversal and revision of the given:
just as scarce resources are made abundant, legitimate power
deemed only weakness, and facts displaced by revealed truth,
so the onetime moment at which *zekhut* is attained from heaven
outweighs a lifetime of Torah learning. *Zekhut* formed the foundation for the Yerushalmi's conception of political economy for
the social order of Israel. It and not Torah defined the whole,
of which economics and politics comprised mere details. It sets
forth and accounts for an economics and a politics that made
powerlessness into power, disinheritance into wealth. How in
fact does *zekhut* function?

Zekhut is gained for a person by an act of renunciation and
self-abnegation, such that heaven responds with an act of grace.
Zekhut is a work of supererogation, which heaven cannot compel
but highly prizes; *zekhut* defines the very opposite of coercion. It
is an act that no one could anticipate or demand, an act of such
remarkable selflessness that heaven finds itself constrained to
respond. That is why the systemic center is formed by an act, on
heaven's part, of responsive grace, meaning, grace one by definition cannot demand or compel but only provoke. When we
make ourselves less, heaven makes us more; but we cannot force
our will upon heaven. When we ask about the femininization of
Judaism, our attention rests upon this fact: the right relationship between Israel and God is not coerced, is not manipulated,
is not defined by a dominant party for a subordinated one. It
is a relationship of mutuality, negotiation, response to what is
freely given through what cannot be demanded but only vol-
unteered. The relationship, in other words, is a feminine, not a
masculine, one, when measured by the prevailing, conventional
stereotypes.

Zekhut intervenes where heaven cannot force its will upon us.
It is that exquisite balance between our will and heaven's will
that, in the end, brings to its perfect balance and entire fulfillment the exploration of the conflict of God's will and our will
that began with Adam and Eve at their last hour in Eden, and
our first hour on earth. And, in context, the fact that we may

inherit a treasury of *zekhut* from our ancestors logically follows: just as we inherit the human condition of the freedom to practice rebellion against God's word, so we inherit, from former generations, the results of another dimension of the human condition: our power to give willingly what none, even God, can by right or rule compel.

This is why the structure of Israel's political economy rested upon divine response to acts of will consisting of submission, on one's own, to the will of heaven; these acts endowed Israel with a lien and entitlement upon heaven. What we cannot by our own will impose, we can by the act of renunciation of our own will evoke. What we cannot accomplish through coercion, we can achieve through submission. God will do for us what we cannot do for ourselves, when we do for God what God cannot make us do. And this means, in a wholly concrete and tangible sense, love God with all the heart, the soul, the might we have. God then stands above the rules of the created world — God will respond not only to what we do in conformity to the rules but also and especially to what we do beyond the requirement of the rules. God is above the rules, and we can gain a response from God when, on some one, unique occasion, we too do more than obey — and love, spontaneously and all at once, with the whole of our being. This is the conception of God that *zekhut*, as a conception of power in heaven and power in humanity, contains. In the relationship between God and humanity expressed in the conception of *Zekhut*, we reach the understanding of what the Torah means when it tells us that we are in God's image and after God's likeness: we are, then, "in our image," the very mirror image of God. God's will forms the mirror image of ours: when we are humble, God responds; when we demand, God withdraws.

The story about Adda bar Ahwah, cited in chapter 2, shows us how *zekhut* surpasses Torah study. For what the sage did to gain such remarkable *zekhut* is not to master such-and-so many tractates of the Mishnah. It was rather acts of courtesy, consideration, gentility, restraint: *cortesía* in the Spanish sense, *gentilezza* in the Italian. These produced *zekhut*. Now all of these acts exhibit in common the virtue of self-abnegation or the avoidance of power over others; they exhibit the submission to the will, and the requirement of self-esteem, of others. Torah study, then, is simply an item on a list of actions or attitudes that generate *zekhut.*

Zekhut as Systemic Center

When we come to a word that is critical to the system of those who use it and also that is beyond translation by a single, exact counterpart in some other language, we know that we have reached the systemic center, the point at which what the system wishes to say is profoundly particular to that system. *Zekhut*[1] in fact refers to two distinct matters: first, virtue that originates with one's ancestors and that is received from them as a legacy, that is, "original virtue"; second, power that heaven accords to people themselves in response to uncoerced acts of grace done by those people. *Zekhut* then is as scarce or common as our capacity for uncoerced action, as strong or weak as our strength to refrain from deeds of worldly power. *Zekhut* accomplished the systemic integration of the successor-documents.

It must follow that *zekhut,* not Torah, in a single word defines the generative myth, the critical symbol of the successor-Judaism. The signal that the study of the Torah formed a mere component in a system that transcended Torah study and defined its structure in some way other than by appeal to the symbol and activity of the Torah comes from a simple fact. Ordinary folk, not disciples of sages, have access to *zekhut* entirely

---

1. The commonly used single word "merit" does not apply as a translation of *zekhut* since "merit" bears the sense of reward for carrying out an obligation: for example, by doing such-and-such, he merited so-and-so. *Zekhut,* by contrast, commonly refers to acts of supererogatory freewill, and therefore while such acts are meritorious in the sense of being virtuous, they are not acts that one owes but that one gives. And the rewards that accumulate in response to such actions are always miraculous or supernatural or signs of divine grace: for example, an unusually long life or the power to prevent a dilapidated building from collapsing. Note the fine perception of S. Levy, *Original Virtue and Other Studies* (London, 1903), 2–3: "Some act of obedience, constituting the Ascent of man, is the origin of virtue and the cause of reward for virtue.... What is the conspicuous act of obedience which, in Judaism, forms the striking contrast to Adam's act of disobedience, in Christianity? The submission of Isaac in being bound on the altar...is regarded in Jewish theology as the historic cause of the imputation of virtue to his descendants."

outside of study of the Torah. In some stories, as noted above, a single remarkable deed, exemplary for its deep humanity, sufficed to win for an ordinary person the *zekhut* that elicits the same marks of supernatural favor enjoyed by some rabbis on account of their Torah study.

Accordingly, the systemic centrality of *zekhut* in the structure, the critical importance of the heritage of virtue together with its supernatural entitlements — these emerge in a striking claim. It is framed in extreme form (another mark of the unique place of *zekhut* within the system): even though a man is degraded, one action can suffice to win for him that heavenly glory to which rabbis in lives of Torah study aspired. The mark of the system's integration around *zekhut* lies in its insistence that all Israelites, not only sages, could gain *zekhut* for themselves (and their descendants).

The Narratives of *Zekhut*

When we come to the way in which *zekhut* is set forth, we find ourselves in a set of narratives of a rather special order. What is special about them is that women play a critical role, appear as heroines, and win the attention and respect of the reader or listener. It is difficult to locate in rabbinic literature before the Talmud of the Land of Israel — the Mishnah, the Tosefta, the Sifra, for instance — stories in which women figure at all. So to take up a whole series of stories in which women are key-players comes as a surprise. But there is more. The storyteller makes the man the hero, on the surface; he is the center of the narrative. And yet a second glance at what is coming shows us that the woman precipitates the tale, and her action, not the man's, represents the gift that cannot be compelled but only given; she is the one who freely sacrifices, and she is also represented as the source of wisdom. So our systemic reversal — that something above the Torah and the study of the Torah takes priority — is matched by a still less predictable shift in narrative quality, with women portrayed as principal actors.

In the instances that follow — each defining what the individual must do to gain *zekhut* — the point is that the deeds of the heroes of the story make them worthy of having their prayers answered, which is a mark of the working of *zekhut*. Supererogatory, uncoerced deeds — those well beyond the strict requirements of the Torah and even the limits of the law altogether — transform the hero into a holy man, whose holiness serves just like that of a sage marked as such by knowledge of the Torah. The following stories should not be understood as expressions of the mere sentimentality of the clerks concerning the lower orders, for they deny, in favor of a single action of surpassing power, sages' lifelong devotion to what the sages held to be the highest value, knowledge of the Torah.

> F. A certain man came before one of the relatives of R. Yannai. He said to him, "Rabbi, attain *zekhut* through me [by giving me charity]."
>
> G. He said to him, "And didn't your father leave you money?"
>
> H. He said to him, "No."
>
> I. He said to him, "Go and collect what your father left in deposit with others."
>
> J. He said to him, "I have heard concerning property my father deposited with others that it was gained by violence [so I don't want it]."
>
> K. He said to him, "You are worthy of praying and having your prayers answered." (Y. Taan. 1:4.1)

The point of K, of course, is self-evidently a reference to the possession of entitlement to supernatural favor, and it is gained, we see, through deeds that the law of the Torah cannot require but must favor. So an act that generates *zekhut* for the individual is the opposite of sin, but it is also its counterpart: both involve doing something of one's own volition that also is beyond all requirements of the law.

In the continuation of this story, we should not miss an odd fact. The story tells about the *zekhut* attained by a humble, poor, ignorant man. It is narrated to underline what he has done. But what provokes the event is an act of self-abnegation far greater than that willingly performed by the male hero — the woman is ready to sell herself into prostitution to save her husband. This is not a focus of the story but the given. Nothing has compelled the woman to surrender her body to save her husband; to the contrary, the marital obligations of a woman concern only conventional deeds (notwithstanding the fact that the Mishnah's law maintains that these deeds may be coerced, and failure to do these deeds may result in financial penalties inflicted on the woman in the settlement of her marriage contract). So the story of the uncoerced act of selflessness is told about a man but occasioned by a woman, and both actors in the story exhibit one and the same virtue.

When Torah stories are told, by contrast, the point is that a man attains *zekhut* by study of the Torah, and a woman attains *zekhut* by sending her sons and her husband off to study the Torah and by sitting home alone — not exactly commensurate action. Only *zekhut* stories like that which follows represent the act of the woman as the counterpart and equivalent to the act of the man; and, in fact, even here, the fact that the woman's uncoerced gift is far greater than the man's — her body, merely his ass — should not go unnoticed. Once more, we find ourselves at the systemic center, where everything is reversed:

L. A certain ass-driver appeared before the rabbis [the context requires: in a dream] and prayed, and rain came. The rabbis sent and brought him and said to him, "What is your trade?"

M. He said to them, "I am an ass-driver."

N. They said to him, "And how do you conduct your business?"

O. He said to them, "One time I rented my ass to a certain woman, and she was weeping on the way, and I said to her, 'What's with you?' and she said to me, 'The husband of that woman [me] is in prison [for debt], and I wanted to see what I can do to free him.' So I sold my ass and I gave her the proceeds, and I said to her, 'Here is your money, free your husband, but do not sin [by becoming a prostitute to raise the necessary funds].' "

P. They said to him, "You are worthy of praying and having your prayers answered." (Y. Tan. 1:4.1)

The ass-driver clearly has a powerful lien on heaven, so that his prayers are answered, even while those of others are not. What did he do to get that entitlement? He did what no law could demand: impoverished himself to save the woman from a "fate worse than death."

Q. In a dream of R. Abbahu, Mr. Pentakaka ["Mr. Five Sins"] appeared, who prayed that rain would come, and it rained. R. Abbahu sent and summoned him. He said to him, "What is your trade?"

R. He said to him, "Five sins does that man [I] do every day, [for I am a pimp:] hiring whores, cleaning up the theater, bringing home their garments for washing, dancing, and performing before them."

S. He said to him, "And what sort of decent thing have you ever done?"

T. He said to him, "One day that man [I] was cleaning the theater, and a woman came and stood behind a pillar and cried. I said to her, 'What's with you?' And she said to me, 'That woman's [my] husband is in prison, and I wanted to see what I can do to free him,' so I sold my bed and cover, and I gave the proceeds to her. I said to her, 'Here is your money, free your husband, but do not sin.'"

U. He said to him, "You are worthy of praying and having your prayers answered." (Y. Tan. 1:4.1)

Point Q moves us still further, since the man has done everything sinful that one can do, and, more to the point, he does it every day. So the act of *zekhut*, which suffices if done only one time, is powerful enough to outweigh a life of sin — again, an act of *zekhut* as the mirror image and opposite of sin. And here again, the single act of saving a woman from a "fate worse than death" has sufficed. The text continues:

V. A pious man from Kefar Imi appeared [in a dream] to the rabbis. He prayed for rain and it rained. The rabbis went up to him. His householders told them that he was sitting on a hill. They went out to him, saying to him, "Greetings," but he did not answer them.

W. He was sitting and eating, and he did not say to them, "You break bread too."

X. When he went back home, he made a bundle of faggots and put his cloak on top of the bundle [instead of on his shoulder].

Y. When he came home, he said to his household [wife], "These rabbis are here [because] they want me to pray for rain. If I pray and it rains, it is a disgrace for them, and if not, it is a profanation of the Name of Heaven. But come, you and I will go up [to the roof] and pray. If it rains, we shall tell them, 'We are not worthy to pray and have our prayers answered.'"

Z. They went up and prayed and it rained.

AA. They came down to them [and asked], "Why have the rabbis troubled themselves to come here today?"

BB. They said to him, "We wanted you to pray so that it would rain."

CC. He said to them, "Now do you really need my prayers? Heaven already has done its miracle."

DD. They said to him, "Why, when you were on the hill, did we say hello to you, and you did not reply?"

EE. He said to them, "I was then doing my job. Should I then interrupt my concentration [on my work]?"

FF. They said to him, "And why, when you sat down to eat, did you not say to us, 'You break bread too'?"

GG. He said to them, "Because I had only my small ration of bread. Why would I have invited you to eat by way of mere flattery [when I knew I could not give you anything at all]?"

HH. They said to him, "And why when you came to go down, did you put your cloak on top of the bundle?"

II. He said to them, "Because the cloak was not mine. It was borrowed for use at prayer. I did not want to tear it."

JJ. They said to him, "And why, when you were on the hill, did your wife wear dirty clothes, but when you came down from the mountain, did she put on clean clothes?"

KK. He said to them, "When I was on the hill, she put on dirty clothes, so that no one would gaze at her. But when I came home from the hill, she put on clean clothes, so that I would not gaze on any other woman."

LL. They said to him, "It is well that you pray and have your prayers answered." (Y. Tan. 1:4.1)

Here the woman is at least an equal player; her actions, as much as her husband's, prove exemplary and illustrate the ultimate wisdom. The pious man of section V finally enjoys the recognition of the sages by reason of his lien upon heaven, able as he is to pray and bring rain. What has so endowed him with *zekhut?* Acts of punctiliousness of a moral order: concentrating on his work, avoiding an act of dissimulation, integrity in the disposition of a borrowed object, his wife's concern not to attract other men, and her equal concern to make herself attractive to her husband.

We note again that at the systemic center women find entire equality with men; with no role whatever in the study of the Torah and no possibility of attaining political sagacity, women find a critical place in the sequence of actions that elicit from heaven the admiring response that *zekhut* embodies. It follows, once more, that those reversals that signal the systemic center culminate in the ultimate reversal: woman at the height (for so male a system as this one). Just as Torah learning is subordinated, so man is subordinated; *zekhut,* the gift that, like love, can be given but not compelled, must be called the female virtue that sits atop a male system and structure.

At M. Sotah 3:4–5 we find for the first time in rabbinic literature clear indication of the presence of a conception of an entitlement deriving from some source other than one's own deed of the moment:

3:4. E. There is the possibility that *zekhut* suspends the curse for one year, and there is the possibility that *zekhut* suspends the curse for two years, and there is the possibility that *zekhut* suspends the curse for three years.

   F. On this basis Ben Azzai says, "A man is required to teach Torah to his daughter.

   G. "For if she should drink the water, she should know that [if nothing happens to her], *zekhut* is what suspends [the curse from taking effect]."

3:5. A. R. Simeon says, "*Zekhut* does not suspend the effects of the bitter water.

B. "And if you say, '*Zekhut* does suspend the effects of the bitter water,' you will weaken the effect of the water for all the
women who have to drink it.

C. "And you give a bad name to all the women who drink it who
turned out to be pure.

D. "For people will say, 'They are unclean, but *zekhut* suspended
the effects of the water for them.' "

E. Rabbi says, "*Zekhut* does suspend the effects of the bitter water.
But she will not bear children or continue to be pretty. And
she will waste away, and in the end she will have the same
[unpleasant] death." (M. Sotah 3:4–5)

Now if we insert "the heritage of virtue and its consequent entitlements" for *zekhut* at each point (thus: "For people will say,
'They are unclean, but the heritage of virtue and its consequent
entitlements suspended the effects of the water for them' "), we
have good sense. That is to say, the reason the woman may not
suffer the penalty to which she is presumably condemnable is
not because her act or condition (for example, her innocence)
has secured her acquittal or nullified the effects of the ordeal
but because she enjoys some advantage extrinsic to her own
act or condition. She may be guilty, but she may also possess
a benefice coming by inheritance, hence, heritage of virtue, and
so be entitled to a protection not because of her own but because
of someone else's action or condition. Once more, when it comes
to *zekhut*, the canonical writings find themselves constrained to
state matters in terms of woman's, not man's, virtue. No one
imagines a woman can attain heaven's favor by Torah study;
but she enjoys, equally with men, the inheritance of unearned
merit. At Abot 2:2 we find the following:

C. "And all who work with the community — let them work with
them for the sake of heaven.

D. "For the [1] *zekhut* of their fathers strengthens them, and their
[fathers'] [2] righteousness stands forever.

E. "And as for you, I credit you with a great reward, as if you had
done [all of the work required by the community on your own
merit alone]."

Here there is no meaning possible other than that given above:
"the heritage of virtue and its consequent entitlements." The

reference to an advantage that one gains by reason of inheritance out of one's fathers' righteousness is demanded by the parallel between *zekhut* of clause [1] and *righteousness* of clause [2]. The sense in the following is still clearer, that *zekhut* is the opposite of sin; as there was original sin, so there is original *zekhut:*

A. He who causes *zekhut* to the community never causes sin.

B. And he who causes the community to sin — they never give him a sufficient chance to attain penitence. (Abot 5:18)

Here the contrast is between causing *zekhut* and causing sin, so *zekhut* is the opposite of sin. The continuation is equally clear: a person attained *zekhut* and endowed the community with *zekhut*, or sinned and made the community sin:

C. Moses attained *zekhut* and bestowed *zekhut* on the community.

D. So the *zekhut* of the community is assigned to his [credit],

E. as it is said, "He executed the justice of the Lord and his judgments with Israel" (Deut. 33:21).

F. Jeroboam sinned and caused the community to sin.

G. So the sin of the community is assigned to his [debit],

H. as it is said, "For the sins of Jeroboam which he committed and wherewith he made Israel to sin" (1 Kings 15:30).

The appropriateness of interpreting the passage in the way proposed will now be shown to be self-evident. All that is required is to substitute for *zekhut* the proposed translation:

C. Moses attained the heritage of virtue and bestowed its consequent entitlements on the community.

D. So the heritage of virtue and its entitlements enjoyed by the community are assigned to his [credit].

The sense, then, is simple. Moses through actions of his own (of an unspecified sort) acquired *zekhut*, which is the credit for such actions that accrued to him and that bestowed upon him certain supernatural entitlements; and he for his part passed on as an inheritance that credit, a lien on heaven for the performance of these same supernatural entitlements: *zekhut*, pure and simple.

Original sin is then matched by original virtue, inherited with the human condition.

This conception of *zekhut* as original virtue is broadened in the later documents into the deeply historical notion of *zekhut abot*, empowerment of a supernatural character to which Israel is entitled by reason of what the patriarchs and matriarchs in particular did long ago. It forms the foundation for the paramount sense of *zekhut* in the successor-system: the Israelite possesses a lien upon heaven by reason of God's love for the patriarchs and matriarchs, his appreciation for certain things they did, and his response to those actions not only in favoring them but also in entitling their descendants to do or benefit from otherwise unattainable miracles. Within the historically grounded metaphor of Israel as a family, a metaphor expressed by the conception of *zekhut abot*, Israel was the children of Abraham, Isaac, and Jacob, or children of Israel, in a concrete and genealogical sense. Israel hence fell into the genus *family* as the particular species of family generated by Abraham and Sarah. The distinguishing trait of that species was that it possessed the inheritance, or heritage, of the patriarchs and matriarchs, and that inheritance, consisting of *zekhut*, served the descendants and heirs as protection and support. It follows that the systemic position of the conception of *zekhut*, to begin with, gives it the power to define the social entity, and hence *zekhut* (in the terms of the initial philosophical category formation) forms a fundamentally political conception and only secondarily an economic and philosophical one.

But *zekhut* serves, in particular, the category that speaks against illegitimate violence, that speaks not of power but of weakness. In context, time and again, we observe that *zekhut* is the power of the weak. People who through their own merit and capacity can accomplish nothing, can accomplish miracles through what others do for them in leaving a heritage of *zekhut*. And, not to miss the stunning message of the triplet of stories cited above, *zekhut* is also what the weak and excluded and despised can do that outweighs in power what the great masters of the Torah have accomplished. In the context of a system that represents Torah as supernatural, the claim of priority for *zekhut* represents a considerable transvaluation of power, as much as of value. And *zekhut* also forms the inheritance of the disinherited: what one receives as a heritage when one has nothing in the present and has gotten nothing in the past; *zekhut* is a scarce resource that is free and unearned but much valued. So let us dwell upon the definitiveness of the transferability of *zekhut* in its formulation *zekhut abot* (the *zekhut* handed on by the ancestors), the transitive character of the concept, and its standing as a heritage of entitlements.

It is in the successor-documents that the concept of *zekhut* is joined with *abot*. The *zekhut* that has been left as Israel's family inheritance by the patriarchs or ancestors yields a very specific notion that defines the systemic politics of Israel; it also yields a theory of Israel not as a (mere) community (e.g., as in tractate Abot's reference to Moses' bestowing *zekhut* upon the community) but as a family, with a history that takes the form of a genealogy, precisely as Genesis has represented that history. Now *zekhut* was joined to the metaphor of the genealogy of patriarchs and matriarchs, and served to form the missing link, explaining how the inheritance and heritage were transmitted from them to their heirs. Consequently, the family, called "Israel," could draw upon the family estate, consisting of the inherited *zekhut* of matriarchs and patriarchs, in such a way as to benefit today from the heritage of yesterday. This notion involved very concrete problems. If "Israel, the family," sinned, it could call upon the *zekhut* accumulated by Abraham and Isaac at the binding of Isaac (Genesis 22) to win forgiveness for that sin. True, "fathers will not die on account of the sin of the sons," but the children may benefit from the *zekhut* of the forebears. This concrete expression of the larger metaphor imparted a practical consequence, moral and theological, that was not at all neglected.

A survey of Genesis Rabbah — other Midrash compilations of the same group can yield equally interesting results — indicates the character and use of the doctrine of *zekhut* because that systematic reading of the book of Genesis dealt with the founders of the family and made explicit the definition of Israel as family. *Zekhut* draws in its wake the notion of the inheritance of an ongoing (historical) family, that of Abraham and Sarah, and *zekhut* worked itself out in the moments of crisis of that fam-

ily in its larger affairs. So the Israelites later on enjoy enormous
zekhut through the deeds of the patriarchs and matriarchs. That
conception comes to expression in what follows:

2. A. " ... [F]or with only my staff I crossed this Jordan, and now I
      have become two companies":

   B. R. Judah bar Simon in the name of R. Yohanan: "In the Torah,
      in the Prophets, and in the Writings we find proof that the
      Israelites were able to cross the Jordan only on account of the
      zekhut achieved by Jacob:

   C. "In the Torah: ' ... [F]or with only my staff I crossed this
      Jordan, and now I have become two companies.'

   D. "In the Prophets: 'Then you shall let your children know, say-
      ing, "Israel came over this Jordan on dry land"' (Josh. 4:22),
      meaning our father, Israel.

   E. "In the Writings: 'What ails you, O you sea, that you flee? You
      Jordan, that you turn backward? At the presence of the God of
      Jacob ...'" (Ps. 114:5ff.). (Gen. Rab. 76:5)

Here is a perfect illustration of the definition of *zekhut* as an
entitlement one may enjoy by reason of what someone else — an
ancestor — has done; and that entitlement involves supernatural
power. Jacob did not only leave *zekhut* as an estate to his heirs.
The process is reciprocal and ongoing. *Zekhut* coming from the
ancestors had helped Jacob himself:

   A. "When the man saw that he did not prevail against Jacob, [he
      touched the hollow of his thigh, and Jacob's thigh was put out
      of joint as he wrestled with him]" (Gen. 32:25):

   B. Said R. Hinena bar Isaac, "[God said to the angel,] 'He is com-
      ing against you with five "amulets" hung on his neck, that is,
      his own *zekhut*, the *zekhut* of his father and of his mother and
      of his grandfather and of his grandmother.

   C. " 'Check yourself out, can you stand up against even his own
      zekhut [let alone the *zekhut* of his parents and grandparents]?'

   D. "The matter may be compared to a king who had a savage dog
      and a tame lion. The king would take his son and sick him
      against the lion, and if the dog came to have a fight with the
      son, he would say to the dog, 'The lion cannot have a fight
      with him, are you going to make out in a fight with him?'

E. "So if the nations come to have a fight with Israel, the Holy One, blessed be he, says to them, 'Your angelic prince could not stand up to Israel, and as to you, how much the more so!'" (Gen. Rab. 77:3.3)

The collectivity of *zekhut*, not only its transferability, is illustrated here: what an individual does confers *zekhut* on the social entity. Moreover, it is a matter of the legitimate exercise of supernatural power. And the reciprocity of the process extended in all directions. Accordingly, what we have in hand is first and foremost a matter of the exercise of legitimate violence, hence a political power. *Zekhut* might project not only backward, coming from an ancestor and serving a descendant, but forward as well. The inner polemic is that the *zekhut* of Jacob and Joseph would more than suffice to overcome Esau. Not only so, but Joseph survived because of the *zekhut* of his ancestors:

A. "She caught him by his garment, ... but he left his garment in her hand and fled and got out of the house. [And when she saw that he had left his garment in her hand and had fled out of the house, she called to the men of her household and said to them, 'See he has brought among us a Hebrew to insult us; he came in to me to lie with me, and I cried out with a loud voice, and when he heard that I lifted up my voice and cried, he left his garment with me and fled and got out of the house']" (Gen. 39:13–15):

B. He escaped through the *zekhut* of the fathers, in line with this verse: "And he brought him forth outside" (Gen. 15:5).

C. Simeon of Qitron said, "It was on account of bringing up the bones of Joseph that the sea was split: 'The sea saw it and fled' (Ps. 114:3), on the *zekhut* of this act, namely: '... and fled and got out.'" (Gen. Rab. 87:8.1)

Zekhut, we see, is both personal and national. Point B refers to Joseph's enjoying the *zekhut* he had inherited; C refers to Israel's enjoying the *zekhut* that they gained through their supererogatory loyalty to that same *zekhut*-rich personality. It specifies what later benefit to the heir, Israel the family, came from which particular action of a patriarch or matriarch.

A. "And Abram gave him a tenth of everything" (Gen. 14:20):

B. R. Judah in the name of R. Nehorai: "On the strength of that blessing the three great pegs on which the world depends, Abraham, Isaac, and Jacob, derived sustenance.

C. "Abraham: 'And the Lord blessed Abraham in *all* things' (Gen. 24:1) on account of the *zekhut* that 'he gave him a tenth of *all* things' (Gen. 14:20).

D. "Isaac: 'And I have eaten of *all*' (Gen. 27:33) on account of the *zekhut* that 'he gave him a tenth of *all* things'" (Gen. 14:20). (Gen. Rab. 43:8.2)

E. "Jacob: 'Because God has dealt graciously with me and because I have all' (Gen. 33:11) on account of the *zekhut* that 'he gave him a tenth of *all* things' (Gen. 14:20).

A. Whence did Israel gain the *zekhut* of receiving the blessing of the priests?

B. R. Judah said, "It was from Abraham: 'So shall your seed be' (Gen. 15:5), while it is written in connection with the priestly blessing: 'So shall you bless the children of Israel'" (Num. 6:23).

C. R. Nehemiah said, "It was from Isaac: 'And I and the lad will go *so* far' (Gen. 22:5); therefore said the Holy One, blessed be he, 'So shall you bless the children of Israel'" (Num. 6:23).

D. And rabbis say, "It was from Jacob: 'So shall you say to the house of Jacob' (Exod. 19:3) (in line with the statement, 'So shall you bless the children of Israel')" (Num. 6:23). (Gen. Rab. 43:8.3)

The first excerpt above (43:8.2) links the blessing at hand with the history of Israel. The reference to the word "all" joins the tithe of Abram to the blessing of his descendants. Since the blessing of the priest is at hand, the second excerpt (43:8.3) treats the origins of the blessing. The picture is clear. "Israel" constitutes a family as a genealogical and juridical fact. It inherits the estate of the ancestors. It hands on that estate. It lives by the example of the matriarchs and patriarchs, and its history exemplifies events in their lives. And *zekhut* forms the entitlement that one generation may transmit to the next, in a way in which the heritage of sin is not to be transmitted except by reason of the deeds of the successor-generation. The good that one does lives onward; the evil is interred with one's bones.

To conclude this brief survey of *zekhut* as the medium of historical existence, that is, the *zekhut* coming from the patriarchs, or *zekhut abot*, let me present a statement of the legitimate power — sufficient to achieve salvation, which, in this context, always bears a political dimension — imparted by the *zekhut* of the ancestors. This *zekhut* will enable them to accomplish the political goals of Israel: attaining self-rule and avoiding government by Gentiles. This statement appeals to the binding of Isaac as the source of the *zekhut* coming from the patriarchs and matriarchs, which will in the end lead to the salvation of Israel. What is important here is that the *zekhut* one inherits joins together with the *zekhut* of one's own deeds; one inherits the *zekhut* of the past, and, moreover, if one does what the progenitors did, one not only receives an entitlement out of the past but also secures an entitlement on one's own account. So the difference between *zekhut* and sin lies in the sole issue of transmissibility:

A. Said R. Isaac, "And all was on account of the *zekhut* attained by the act of prostration.

B. "Abraham returned in peace from Mount Moriah only on account of the *zekhut* owing to the act of prostration: '[A]nd we will worship [through an act of prostration] and come [then, on that account] again to you' (Gen. 22:5).

C. "The Israelites were redeemed only on account of the *zekhut* owing to the act of prostration: 'And the people believed; ...then they bowed their heads and prostrated themselves' (Exod. 4:31).

D. "The Torah was given only on account of the *zekhut* owing to the act of prostration: 'And worship [through prostration] you afar off' (Exod. 24:1).

E. "Hannah was remembered only on account of the *zekhut* owing to the act of prostration: 'And they worshiped before the Lord' (1 Sam. 1:19).

F. "The exiles will be brought back only on account of the *zekhut* owing to the act of prostration: 'And it shall come to pass in that day that a great horn shall be blown and they shall

come that were lost...and that were dispersed,...and they
shall worship the Lord in the holy mountain at Jerusalem' (Isa.
27:13).

G. "The Temple was built only on account of the *zekhut* owing to
the act of prostration: 'Exalt you the Lord our God and worship
at his holy hill' (Ps. 99:9).

H. "The dead will live only on account of the *zekhut* owing to the
act of prostration: 'Come let us worship and bend the knee,
let us kneel before the Lord our maker'" (Ps. 95:6). (Gen. Rab.
56:2.5)

The entire history of Israel flows from its acts of worship
(prostration) beginning with what Abraham performed at the
binding of Isaac. Every sort of advantage Israel has ever gained
came about through that act of worship done by Abraham and
imitated thereafter. Israel constitutes a family and inherits the
zekhut laid up as a treasure for the descendants by the ancestors. It draws upon that *zekhut*, but, by doing the deeds they
did, it also enhances its heritage of *zekhut* and leaves to its descendants greater entitlement than they would enjoy by reason
of their own actions. But their own actions — here, prostration
in worship — generate *zekhut* as well.

Accordingly, *zekhut* is as much personal as it is inherited and
collective. The *zekhut* coming from the prior generations is collective and affects all Israel. But one's own deeds can generate
zekhut for oneself. Specifically, Jacob reflects on the power that
Esau's own *zekhut* had gained for Esau. He had gained that
zekhut by living in the Land of Israel and also by paying honor
and respect to Isaac. Jacob then feared that he would not be able
to overcome Esau because of the *zekhut* that Esau had gained. So
zekhut worked on its own; it was a credit gained by proper action, which went to the credit of the person who had done that
action. What made the action worthy of evoking heaven's response of an act of supernatural favor is that it was an action
not to be required, but if done, to be rewarded, an act of will
that cannot be coerced but must be honored. In Esau's case, it
was the simple fact that he had remained in the holy land:

2. A. "Then Jacob was greatly afraid and distressed" (Gen. 32:7):
[This is Jacob's soliloquy:] "Because of all those years that

Esau was living in the Land of Israel, perhaps he may come against me with the power of the *zekhut* he has now attained by dwelling in the Land of Israel.

B. "Because of all those years of paying honor to his father, perhaps he may come against me with the power of the *zekhut* he attained by honoring his father.

C. "So he said: 'Let the days of mourning for my father be at hand, then I will slay my brother Jacob' (Gen. 27:41).

D. "Now the old man is dead." (Gen. Rab. 76:2)

The important point, then, is that *zekhut* is not only inherited as part of a collective estate left by the patriarchs. It is also accomplished by an individual in his or her own behalf. By extension, the successor-system opens a place for recognition of the individual, both man and woman, within the system of *zekhut*. As we shall now see, what a man or a woman does may win for that person an entitlement upon heaven for supernatural favor of some sort. So there is space, in the system, for a private person, and the individual is linked to the social order through the shared possibilities of generating or inheriting an entitlement upon heaven.

Deeds That Generate *Zekhut*

If we now ask, What are the sorts of deeds that generate *zekhut?* we realize that these deeds produce a common result of gaining for their doer, as much as for the heirs of the actor, an entitlement for heavenly favor and support when needed. And this fact concerning gaining and benefiting from *zekhut* brings us to the systemic message to the living generation, the account of what now is to be done. This message proves acutely contemporary, for it stresses the power of a single action to create sufficient *zekhut* to outweigh a life of sin. Then the contrast between sin and *zekhut* gains greater depth still. One sin of sufficient weight condemns; one act of *zekhut* of sufficient weight saves. The entire issue of entitlements out of the past gives way, then, when we realize what is actually at stake.

We recall that Torah study is one — but only one — means for an individual to gain access to that heritage, to get *zekhut*. There are other equally suitable means, and the merit gained by Torah study is no different from the merit gained by acts of a supererogatory character. If one gets *zekhut* for studying the Torah, then we must suppose there is no holy deed that does not generate its share of *zekhut*. But when it comes to specifying the things one does to get *zekhut*, the documents before us speak of what the Torah does not require but does recommend: not what we are commanded to do in detail, but what the right attitude, formed within the Torah, leads us to do of our own volition. What is it that Israelites as a nation do to gain a lien upon heaven for themselves or entitlements of supernatural favor for their descendants? Here is one representative answer to that question:

A. "If the God of my father, the God of Abraham and the Fear of Isaac, had not been on my side, surely now you would have sent me away empty-handed. God saw my affliction and the labor of my hand and rebuked you last night" (Gen. 31:41–42):

B. Zebedee b. Levi and R. Joshua b. Levi:

C. Zebedee said, "Every passage in which reference is made to 'if' tells of an appeal to the *zekhut* accrued by the patriarchs."

D. Said to him R. Joshua, "But it is written, 'Except we had lingered' (Gen. 43:10) [a passage not related to the *zekhut* of the patriarchs]."

E. He said to him, "They themselves would not have come up except for the *zekhut* of the patriarchs, for if it were not for the *zekhut* of the patriarchs, they never would have been able to go up from there in peace."

F. Said R. Tanhuma, "There are those who produce the matter in a different version." [It is given as follows:]

G. R. Joshua and Zebedee b. Levi:

H. R. Joshua said, "Every passage in which reference is made to 'if' tells of an appeal to the *zekhut* accrued by the patriarchs except for the present case."

I. He said to him, "This case too falls under the category of an appeal to the *zekhut* of the patriarchs." (Gen. Rab. 74:12.1)

So much for *zekhut* that is inherited from the patriarchs, a now familiar notion. But what about the deeds of Israel in the here and now?

> J. R. Yohanan said, "It was on account of the *zekhut* achieved through sanctification of the divine name."

> K. R. Levi said, "It was on account of the *zekhut* achieved through faith and the *zekhut* achieved through Torah."

Faith despite the here and now and study of the Torah — Israel gains an entitlement for themselves or their heirs by practicing these in the here and now.

> L. "The *zekhut* achieved through faith: 'If I had not believed...' (Ps. 27:13).

> M. "The *zekhut* achieved through Torah: 'Unless your Torah had been my delight...'" (Ps. 119:92).

> 2. A. "God saw my affliction and the labor of my hand and rebuked you last night" (Gen. 31:41–42):

> B. Said R. Jeremiah b. Eleazar, "More beloved is hard labor than the *zekhut* achieved by the patriarchs, for the *zekhut* achieved by the patriarchs served to afford protection for property only, while the *zekhut* achieved by hard labor served to afford protection for lives.

> C. "The *zekhut* achieved by the patriarchs served to afford protection for property only: 'If the God of my father, the God of Abraham and the Fear of Isaac, had not been on my side, surely now you would have sent me away empty-handed.'

> D. "The *zekhut* achieved by hard labor served to afford protection for lives: 'God saw my affliction and the labor of my hand and rebuked you last night.'"

Here is as good an account as any of the theology of *zekhut*. The issue of the *zekhut* of the patriarchs comes up in the reference to the God of the fathers. The conception of the *zekhut* of the patriarchs is explicit, not general. It specifies what later benefit to the heir, Israel the family, came from which particular action of a patriarch or matriarch. But acts of faith and Torah study form only one medium; hard labor, that is, devotion to one's calling, defines the source of *zekhut* that is going to be accessible to those many Israelites unlikely to distinguish themselves either by Torah study and acts of faith, encompassing the sanctification of God's name, or by acts of amazing gentility and restraint.

The system here speaks to everybody, Jew and Gentile, past and present and future; *zekhut* therefore defines the structure of the cosmic social order and explains how it is supposed to function. It is the encompassing quality of *zekhut*, its pertinence to past and future, high and low, rich and poor, gifted and ordinary, that marks the message of *zekhut* as the systemic statement: *zekhut* is now fully revealed as the conception of reciprocal response between heaven and Israel on earth and as being constituted by acts of devotion beyond the requirements of the Torah but defined all the same by the Torah. As Scripture had said, God responds to the faith of the ancient generations by supernatural acts to which, on their own account, the moderns are not entitled, hence a heritage of entitlement. But those acts, now fully defined for us, can and ought to be done, also, by the living generation. And, as a matter of fact, no one today, or at the time of the system builders, is exempt from the systemic message and its demands: even steadfastness in accomplishing the humble work of the everyday and the here and now.

The systemic statement made by the usages of *zekhut* speaks of relationship, function, and the interplay of humanity and God. One's store of *zekhut* comes from a relationship, that is, from one's forebears. This is one dimension of the relationships in which one stands. *Zekhut* also forms a measure of one's own relationship with heaven, as the power of one person, but not another, to pray and so bring rain attests. What sort of relationship does *zekhut*, as the opposite of sin, then posit? It is not one of coercion, for heaven cannot force us to do those types of deeds that yield *zekhut*, and this, story after story suggests, is the definition of a deed that generates *zekhut:* doing what we ought to do but do not have to do. But then we cannot coerce heaven to do what we want done either, for example, by carrying out the commandments. These are obligatory but do not obligate heaven.

Whence then the lien on heaven? To recapitulate: it is through deeds of a supererogatory character to which heaven responds by deeds of a supererogatory character: supernatural favor to this one, who through deeds of ingratiation of the other or self-abnegation or restraint exhibits the attitude that in heaven precipitates a counterpart attitude, hence generating *zekhut*, rather than to that one, who does not. The simple fact that rabbis cannot pray and bring rain, but a simple ass-driver can, tells the whole story. The relationship measured by *zekhut* contains an element of unpredictability for which appeal to the *zekhut* inherited from ancestors accounts. So while a person cannot coerce heaven, he or she — for women as much as men enjoy full access to *zekhut*, though they do not to the study of the Torah — can through *zekhut* gain acts of favor from heaven by doing what heaven cannot require. Heaven responds to one's attitude in carrying out one's duties — and more than those duties. This act of pure disinterest — for example, the ass-driver giving the woman his means of livelihood — is the one that gains heaven's deepest interest.

Christianity's conceptions of the crucified Messiah, the power of weakness, and the glory of surrender find a counterpart in the concept of *zekhut*. Here we find the ultimate reversal, which the moves from the legitimacy of power to the legitimacy of weakness, in perspective, merely adumbrate. "Make God's wishes yours, so that God will make your wishes his. Anyone from whom people take pleasure, God takes pleasure" (Abot 2:4). These two statements hold together the two principal elements of the conception of the relationship to God that the single word *zekhut* conveys. Give up; please others; do not impose your will but give way to the will of the other — do these and heaven will respond by giving a lien that is not coerced but evoked. By the rationality of discipline within, we have the power to form rational relationships beyond ourselves with heaven; and that is how the system expands the boundaries of the social order to encompass not only the natural but also the supernatural world.

Treating every deed, every gesture, as capable of bringing about enchantment, the successor-system imparted to the givens of everyday life — at least in their potential — remarkable power. The conviction that by dint of special effort one may so conduct himself or herself as to acquire an entitlement of supernatural power turns one's commonplace circumstance into an arena encompassing heaven and earth. God responds to an individual's — and holy Israel's — virtue, filling the gap, so to speak, about oneself and about one's entire family that one leaves when one forbears, withdraws, and gives up what is one's own: one's space, one's self. When one does this, God responds; one's sacrifice then evokes memories of Abraham's readiness to sacrifice Isaac; devotion to the other calls up from heaven what by demanding one cannot coerce. What imparts critical mass to the conception of *zekhut* is the recasting of the political economy of Israel — in the Land of Israel — in the mold and model of the virtue of surrender. This accounts for the definition of legitimate power in politics as only weakness, economics as the rational increase of resources that are, but need not be, scarce, valued things that are capable of infinite increase.

God in the successor-system gains what the philosophical God lacks, which is personality, active presence, pathos, and empathy. The God of the religious system breaks the rules, accords an entitlement to this one, who has done some one remarkable deed, but not to that one, who has done nothing wrong and everything right. So a life in accord with the rules — even a life spent in the study of the Torah — in heaven's view is outweighed by a single moment, a gesture that violates the norm, extending the outer limits of the rule, for instance, of virtue. Only a God who, like us, feels (not only thinks) and responds to impulse and sentiment can be portrayed in such a way as this:

> So I sold my ass and I gave her the proceeds, and I said to her, 'Here is your money, free your husband, but do not sin [by becoming a prostitute to raise the necessary funds].' "
>
> They said to him, "You are worthy of praying and having your prayers answered."

No rule exhaustively describes a world such as this. Here the law of love is transcended, for love itself is now surpassed. Beyond love is the willing, uncoerced sacrifice of self: love of the other more than the love of self, love of the Other most of all. Feminine Judaism relates to God as lovers relate to one another: giving not in order to receive, receiving only in order to give.

What is asked of Israel and of the Israelite individual now is truly godly restraint, supernatural generosity of soul that is "in our image, after our likeness": this is what goes beyond all rules. And since this appeal to transcend the norm defined not personal virtue but the sainthood of all Israel, living all together in the here and now, we must conclude that, within Israel's society, within what the Greco-Roman world will have called its polis, its political and social order, the bounds of earth have now extended to heaven. In terms of another great system composed at the same time and in response to a world-historical catastrophe of the same sort, Israel on earth dwells in the city of God. And, it must follow, God dwells with Israel, in Israel: "today, if you will it."

The Judaism set forth in the successor-documents was a social order in which, while taking full account of circumstance and historical context, individuals and nation alike controlled their own destiny. The circumstance of genealogy dictated whether or not the moral entity, whether the individual or the nation, would enjoy access to entitlements of supernatural favor without regard to merit. But, whether favored by a rich heritage of supernatural empowerment as was the nation, or deprived, by reason of one's immediate ancestors, of any lien upon heaven, in the end both the nation and the individual had in hand the power to shape the future. How was this to be done? It was not alone by keeping the Torah, studying the Torah, dressing, eating, making a living, marrying, procreating, raising a family, burying and being buried, all in accord with those rules.

A life in conformity with the rule, obligatory but merely conventional, does not evoke the special interest of heaven. Why should it? The rules describe the ordinary. In language used only in a later document: "[T]he All-Merciful really wants the heart," and that is not an ordinary thing. Nor was the power to bring rain or hold up a tottering house gained through a life of merely ordinary sanctity. Special favor responded to extraordinary actions, in the analogy of special disfavor, misfortune deemed to punish sin. And just as culpable sin, as distinct from mere error, requires an act of will, specifically, arrogance, so an act of extraordinary character requires an act of will. But, as mirror image of sin, the act would reveal in a concrete way an attitude of restraint, forbearance, gentility, and self-abnegation. A sinful act, provoking heaven, is one that is done deliberately to defy heaven. Thus an act that would evoke heaven's favor, so imposing upon heaven a lien that heaven freely gives, is one that, equally deliberately and concretely, displays humility.

Zekhut is the power of the powerless, the riches of the disinherited, the valuation and valorization of the will of those who have no right to will. *Zekhut* arms Israel with the weapons of woman: the strength of weakness, the power of patience and endurance, the coercion that comes about through surviving, come what may. This feminine Judaism's Israel is a family, its God a lover and beloved, its virtue uncoerced, its wisdom uncompelled — this Judaism served for those long centuries in which Judaism addressed a people that could not dominate but only reason; that could not manipulate but only hope; that could not guarantee results but only trust in what would be. In the context of Christian Palestine, Jews found themselves on the defensive. Their ancestry called into question, their supernatural standing thrown into doubt, their future denied, they called themselves "Israel," and the land, "the Land of Israel." But what power did they possess, legitimately, if need be through violence, to assert their claim to form "Israel"? And, with the holy land passing into the hands of others, what scarce resource did they own that could take the place of that measure of value that now no longer was subjected to their rationality? Asserting a politics in which all violence was illegitimate, an economics in which nothing tangible, even real property in the holy land, had value, the system through its counterpart-categories made a single, simple, and sufficient statement.

Study of the Torah, which only men could do, emerges as contingent; the life of obedience to the commandments proves necessary but not sufficient; Israel's relationship to God finds its definition not in what it must do but in what it alone can decide to do; this is a relationship in which nothing is commanded or coerced or imposed through domination or manipulation. This Judaism values relations that are mutual and negotiated, cooperative, suggestive, not assertive, coercive, or aggressive. The conception of *zekhut* came to the fore to integrate the system's theory of the way of life of the social order, its economics, with its account of the social entity of the social order, its politics. The remarkable actions — perhaps those of omission more than those of commission — that produced *zekhut* yielded an increase in the scarcest of all resources: supernatural favor; and at the same time these actions endowed individuals — persons rich in entitlements to heavenly intervention — with a power to evoke that vastly outweighed the this-worldly power to coerce in the accomplishment of their purposes. It is no wonder that, at the systemic apex, woman and the virtue that is natural to her situation now sit enthroned. The right relationship to God is one of responsive grace and love freely given, one that is not subject to conditions but that embodies perfect commitment.

Part Two

The Bible as God's Word

BRUCE D. CHILTON

4

The Bible in the Church

Christians are nearly unanimous in making the claim that Scripture holds the status of revelation. At the same time, diversity and dispute within Christianity are the predictable outcome when Christians attempt to say how Scripture reveals God. In the Second Letter of Timothy the writer says, in Paul's name, "All Scripture is inspired of God and useful for instruction" (2 Tim. 3:16). The statement has been taken to imply different things. It might imply that God delivered the individual words of Scripture to its writers, or that the writers personally were inspired during the course of their thought, or that Scripture functions to inspire when it is understood and applied properly. Roughly speaking, the first option would be consistent with a fundamentalist stance, the second with a conservative point of view, and the third with a liberal construction of Christianity.

The range of possible readings of 2 Tim. 3:16 could easily be extended, but it is worthwhile to reflect on the three widely represented options that have been mentioned. Each is often taken by partisans of the viewpoint concerned — fundamentalist, conservative, or liberal — to be the plain meaning of the text. Scholars of a given persuasion will argue that theirs is the intended meaning of the text and that other interpretations are suspect. Indeed, many readers of this book will probably have an instant reaction to the words that have been quoted and understand them unequivocally to refer to the verbal inspiration of Scripture, to the inspired nature of biblical writing, or to the inspiring quality of what is written.

The strength of one's conviction that a given meaning is *the* meaning of the text reflects several factors. The most important factor is also the most obvious: how words are understood in their context. Context, however, is far from obvious in the case of any text from the past. Scholarly discussion necessarily focuses on the language, the social and historical setting, and the literary connections involved.

However the context is defined, the second and vital factor to be considered is the cultural stance of the reader. Each of us approaches a work such as the Bible with preunderstandings concerning its significance: some, for example, will say it is the word of God, but others will condemn it as an instrument of oppression, and there are many intermediate positions. The role of preunderstanding is vital in the interpretation of any text, but it need not predetermine our reading. Indeed, critical and intelligent reading occurs when we open for scrutiny both our perception of what a text means within its own context (the first factor) and our cultural preunderstanding within our world (the second factor), and then permit those two factors to interact with each other. The result may be to confirm or to transform our prior understanding of a text's significance.

The interaction between a text's contextual meaning and a reader's cultural stance is frequently influenced by a third factor: social constraints regarding the significance that *should* be found in the text. Some groups insist that to understand the Bible as the word of God implies that error or contradiction must not be referred to. Any such reference amounts to a one-way ticket out of the group. But social constraint is also a determinative factor in other settings. A prominent scholar at Yale University recently informed a graduate seminar that a theological discussion of Paul was not appropriate; his concern was only the social setting of what Paul said. Social constraints of that kind in some cases override considerations of meaning and an interpreter's cultural stance. Ideological imperatives — theological or secular — can and do sometimes impose the meanings that readers are permitted to discover in texts.

In most cases, however, we live in communities that see a correspondence among the three factors (contextual, cultural, and social). The meaning of a formative text in its historical context — it might be the Bible, the *Iliad*, the Talmud, the Constitution of the United States — is held to comport well with the cultural preunderstanding of the reader and with the social constraints of the group. Churches have been especially skillful at balancing that equation of text, individual cognition, and social expectation. That can happen because the Bible is held to be authoritative, although the grounds and the manner of biblical authority are often spelled out differently.

What is currently called postmodernism may be described, where it concerns interpretation, as the recognition that there is no single reading of any classic text, ancient or modern, that can command general assent. In the face of such relativism, Christian appeals to claims of absolute meaning are understandable. Fundamentalism is an authentic (and often a courageous) Christian response to relativism.[1] After all, if meaning may be constructed as the reader wishes, any notion of God would become the textual equivalent of an idol. God in most postmodernist constructions is cast more in our image than we are in God's.

The paradox in which the Church finds itself is that, in order to address postmodern relativism, it reflexively insists upon an absolute; but Christian absolutes seem themselves to be culturally relative. Indeed, the stronger the claim to stand outside the pluralism of values, the more it appears to be an example of how our wider society tolerates unusual, exclusivist perspectives and styles of life. The tension between toleration and truth is acute among many Christians; accordingly many non-Christians caricature the Church as being either blindly dogmatic or too readily accommodating to current fashions.

The postmodernist trap is that Christians can say whatever they like, but the more certain they are of their position, the more they will be dismissed as either no longer religious or an anachronism. Those are the simple rules of doctrine by which postmodernism as a secular dogma justifies a refusal to consider the intellectual substance of the Church's thought. As in the case of most movements of intellectual repression, it is pro-

---

1. Fundamentalism should not be confused with literalism. The purpose of fundamentalist readings is to discover the fundamentals of faith within the Bible. Those basic elements are then used to harmonize discrepancies among texts.

mulgated by intellectuals. Its influence in American universities and colleges is obvious.

Such symptoms of strained relations among claims upon intellectual loyalty are nothing new within the experience of the Church. The fact is that Christian faith has been worked out — not only typically but canonically — within the environment of competing claims to truth. The canon of the New Testament emerged during the course of preaching the significance of Jesus Christ, *before* any consensus had been articulated. One of the few constant factors in the emergence of consensus was a common reference to the Hebrew Bible.

The truth that Christianity claims for its preaching is not an absolute that it claims to have understood from the outset. Its truth is rather felt to precede understanding. The Scriptures of Israel provided a common reference, and the significance of Jesus Christ emerged during the course of interpreting those Scriptures. For that reason, to understand the interpretation of Scripture within the primitive Church is at the same time to apprehend the foundation of Christian authority.

The Bible of the Primitive Church

The New Testament represents different communities within early Christianity and their various approaches to Scripture. But "Scripture" is in each document clearly understood to be the Bible of Judaism, normally in its Greek translation, the Septuagint.

The Letter of Aristeas, which circulated from the second century B.C.E., provides a purported account of how the translation came about:[2] the librarian of the great collection in Alexandria, Demetrius of Phalerum, proposes the project of translating the Jewish law, and his ruler, Ptolemy II Philadelphus (285–247 B.C.E.), agrees. Ptolemy, in turn, requests the help of the high priest in Jerusalem, who sends seventy-two translators to accomplish the project. After the translators are lavishly received

---

2. See R. J. H. Shutt, "The Letter of Aristeas," in *The Old Testament Pseudepigrapha*, ed. J. H. Charlesworth (Garden City, N.Y.: Doubleday, 1985), 2:7–34.

by Ptolemy, they retreat to an island and complete their work in seventy-two days. Throughout Aristeas's narrative, the wisdom of the high priest Eleazar and the seventy-two translators, six from each tribe, is emphasized.

Aristeas's letter is a legendary work, which is widely dated more than a century after the events it refers to. It is not even included in what is called the Apocrypha, the books and portions of the Septuagint that do not have any counterpart in the Hebrew Bible. It was nonetheless widely circulated in antiquity among Jews and Christians.[3] The point of the document is that the Septuagint is both a competent and an inspired translation, warranted by the high priest in sending the seventy-two translators whom he had chosen and by God in enabling them to complete their work with miraculous accord in seventy-two days. Aristeas provides an explanation, in short, of why Jews as well as non-Jews (who traditionally numbered seventy or seventy-two nations) should use the Septuagint with confidence.[4]

Aristeas demonstrates that the Greek milieu in which the New Testament was produced had already seen the claim that Moses, the Prophets, and the Writings (the traditional parts of the Hebrew Bible) could properly be understood in the Greek language. The early Christians would take up that claim, as they — in disparate communities within a pluralistic environment — framed their apprehension of God's action in Christ in and through the language of Scripture. There is a basic coherence in the various approaches that they represent, but no single method of interpretation. In what follows, let us consider some examples of interpretation of Scripture within the New Testament. Each of the instances selected here is typical of many more passages in the New Testament and of an influential approach to Scripture within early Christianity.

---

3. Works that are not canonical but that were nonetheless circulated for religious purposes are commonly referred to as the Pseudepigrapha. They are generally attributed to ancient writers, such as Moses and Job, which accounts for the designation.

4. At a later stage, rabbinic authorities would also accord the Septuagint a position of privilege (see Y. Meg. 1:1).

Paul's Interpretation of Abraham

Paul wrote a letter to a group of churches in the northern part of Asia Minor (present-day Turkey) sometime around 53 C.E.[5] He communicated to communities he himself had founded, where Christians were embroiled in a deep and destructive controversy. As Paul sees the matter,[6] he had established the practice of common fellowship at meals, including eucharistic meals, in churches that he founded. Such fellowship, of course, included Jews who became Christians, signaling their acceptance of Jesus' teaching by being baptized. But it also — and increasingly — saw the participation of non-Jews who had been baptized but not circumcised. Paul won the agreement of Christian leaders in Jerusalem that circumcision should not be required of non-Jewish members.

The remarkable and early agreement that Jews and non-Jews could be included in the movement established a radical principle of inclusion. But it also brought about one of the greatest controversies within the early Church. Paul's version of events is the best available.[7] At Antioch, Jews and non-Jews who had been baptized joined in meals of fellowship together. According to Paul, Peter and Barnabas fell in with the practice. Peter — whom Paul also calls "Cephas," the Aramaic word for "rock" (the nickname came from Jesus himself [see Matt. 16:18]) — was a founding apostle of the church in Jerusalem. Barnabas, a Levite from Cyprus, was a prominent, loyal recruit in Jerusalem who enjoyed the trust of the apostles and mediated relations between them and Paul.[8]

Paul's policy of including Gentiles with Jews in meals, as well as in baptism, needed the support of authorities such as Peter and Barnabas, in order to prevail against the natural conservatism of those for whom such inclusion seemed a be-

---

5. For the dating of documents and the considerations involved, see Bruce Chilton, *Beginning New Testament Study* (London: SPCK, 1986; Grand Rapids: Eerdmans, 1987).

6. His position is set out in chapter 2 of Galatians.

7. Galatians 2, as above, but seconded by Acts 15.

8. See Acts 4:36–37; 9:26–30; 11:19–26. According to Acts 11:22–24, Barnabas was the designated contact between Jerusalem and the increasingly important community in Antioch.

trayal of the purity of Israel. When representatives of James arrived, this natural conservatism reasserted itself. (James was the brother of Jesus and the preeminent figure in the church in Jerusalem.)[9] Peter "separated himself," taking along the rest of the Jews and even Barnabas (Gal. 2:12, 13). Jews and Gentiles again maintained distinct fellowship at meals, and Paul accused the leadership of his own movement of hypocrisy (Gal. 2:13).

The radical quality of Paul's position needs to be appreciated before his characteristic interpretation of Scripture may be understood. He was isolated from every other Christian Jew (in Gal. 2:11–13 he names James, Peter, Barnabas, and "the rest of the Jews"). His isolation required that he develop an alternative view of authority in order to justify his own practice. Within Galatians, Paul quickly articulates the distinctive approach to Scripture as authoritative that characterizes the whole of his writings.

He begins with the position of his readers at the time that they heard the preaching of the gospel of Jesus Christ: Did you receive the spirit from "works of law" or from "hearing with faith" (Gal. 3:2)? The rhetoric of the question grounds Paul's readers in their own experience. They could not, as non-Jews, claim to have been obedient to the law; therefore whatever enabled them to respond to the gospel must have been a matter of God's furnishing his spirit (Gal. 3:5). The experience of Paul's readers at the time they heard the gospel is the explicit groundwork of his approach to the Scriptures.

Paul's letters as a whole were written for communities that had already received the message concerning Jesus Christ and specifically for individuals who had already been baptized. (As we will see, the first three Gospels were written to help to prepare interested persons for baptism.) Given the nature of the literature of the New Testament, it is relatively rare to have a glimpse of what it was like for enthusiastic hearers first to receive the gospel concerning Jesus. Here, however, Paul speaks of Jesus Christ as having been "placarded as crucified" before

---

9. See Mark 6:3 and the presentation of James's authority in Acts 15 (as we are about to see.)

the eyes of the Galatians (3:1); evidently, the crucifixion was a vivid and dramatic moment in Paul's own preaching.

The drama was not merely decorative. Hearing with faith became the occasion on which the Galatians received the spirit, and God performed what Paul calls "powers" in their midst (Gal. 3:5). The nature of those wonders is not spelled out, but from what Paul says elsewhere, it is reasonable to suppose that he understands power as that which raised Jesus from the dead (2 Cor. 13:4) and which enables the individual believer to overcome weakness (2 Cor. 12:6–10). In other words, "power" is what people are endowed with when they receive spirit.

Paul does not refer to spirit or to power by way of argument; he simply assumes that they are part of the common experience of his audience. Early Christians, for all their diversity, made a singular claim in regard to the spirit of God. That same spirit that moved over the face of the waters at the beginning of creation (Gen. 1:2), that animated prophets such as Isaiah (Isa. 61:1), and that descended upon Jesus over the waters of his baptism (Mark 1:10) was claimed by Christians in their baptism. As Paul put it later in Galatians, because we are sons, God sent the spirit of his son into our hearts, crying, "Abba, father" (4:6). We feel what Jesus felt, as Paul says, and we call God "Abba," the Aramaic term used by Jesus.

To a large extent, the New Testament reflects divergences and controversies among communities of Christians that struggled with one another (and sometimes against one another) as their lives of faith developed. For that reason, in this volume we must trace distinctive (and sometimes contradictory) attitudes toward Scripture. But the underlying consensus among early Christians — that hearing the gospel of Jesus with faith endowed one with the spirit and its power — is what unified them and set them apart from other groups. Hellenistic philosophy during the period increasingly emphasized the rational nature of any genuine divinity, while Judaism offered both a reasonable and a traditional account of a single God and his ways. Christians' insistence upon their own consciousness of God's spirit made them seem rather like some of the esoteric movements of the Greco-Roman world that offered initiation into the secrets of a hidden realm. Unlike such movements, which could involve expensive rituals (as in the Mysteries) and expert training (as in Gnosticism), Christianity asserted that God made himself available personally after only a modest initiation. Baptism in Christian preaching held the key to God's spirit and the experience of divine power.

Paul therefore grounds his argument in what may be taken to be a matter of widespread agreement: belief in Jesus Christ endows one with spirit. But he then launches into a polemical point: "Are you so foolish that, having begun with spirit, you will now end with flesh?" (Gal. 3:3). The unexpressed assumption is that the observance of purity, such as the emissaries of James insist upon, is a matter of "flesh," not "spirit." Of course, just that presumption is what separates Paul from James, as well as from Peter, Barnabas, and "the rest of the Jews." What Paul requires in order to sustain his polemic is some convincing demonstration that faith is on the side of spirit and observance on the side of flesh.

Paul finds what he needs in Scripture, namely, in the example of Abraham. He says that when believers hear with faith, they are "just as Abraham, who believed in God, and it was reckoned to him as righteousness" (Gal. 3:6). The characterization of Abraham is taken from Genesis (15:5–6), where Abraham is promised that his descendants shall be as the stars of the heavens. His trust in what he is told makes him the father of faith, and in the course of the sacrifice that he subsequently offers, God seals his promise as the solemn covenant to give the land that would be called Israel (Gen. 15:7–21).

Paul understands the role of Abraham as the patriarch of Judaism, but he argues that Abraham's faith, not his obedience to the law, made him righteous in the sight of God: "Know, therefore, that those who are of faith are sons of Abraham" (Gal. 3:7). Paul was capable of remarkable elaborations of that theme, in Galatians and elsewhere, but the essential simplicity of the thought must not be overlooked. Abraham, for Paul, embodied a principle of believing that was best fulfilled by means of faith in and through Jesus Christ. Descent from Abraham, therefore, was a matter of belief, not a matter of genealogy.

What follows in Galatians is an interpretative tour de force around that theme. Scripture itself is held to attest Paul's own view of Abraham. When Abraham is referred to as a blessing among the nations in Gen. 12:3, that is because Gentiles who live from faith are blessed with Abraham's faith (Gal. 3:8–9, 11). Their blessing is their reception of the spirit in faith. Even at this point, then, Paul's interpretative argument is grounded in an appeal to the nature of Christian experience, especially in baptism.

But Paul's presentation of Abraham is designed to deny the strictures of James, as well as to legitimate his own point of view. "Works of law" did not occasion reception of the spirit; "hearing with faith" did (Gal. 3:2). This dichotomy between faith and law is also a theme within Paul's interpretation of Abraham. Scripture itself, as Paul reads it in Gal. 3:10–12, shows that law is quite different from faith. Deuteronomy says that anyone is cursed who does not abide by everything that is written in the book of the law (27:26), while the prophet Habakkuk insists that a righteous person shall live from faith (2:4). Law cannot be considered unconditional because the same book of Deuteronomy (21:22–23) states that a person who is hanged is to be considered cursed: the very crucifixion that occasioned hearing with faith is condemned by the law! Viewed from the perspective of the law, the crucified Jesus is an outrage; viewed from the perspective of faith, he occasions our endowment with the spirit of God (Gal. 3:14).

The exact terms of the covenant with Abraham confirm the perspective of faith in Paul's interpretation. God directs his promises to Abraham's "seed," in the singular (Gen. 12:7 and elsewhere), as if a particular figure were in mind. That figure, Paul says without argument, is Christ (Gal. 3:16). The law cannot condition that covenantal promise; its function, when it came some four hundred thirty years after the promise, was only to deal with the interim until the seed to whom the promise was given should arrive (Gal. 3:15–22). It is promise that conditions law, rather than the reverse.

Judged from the point of view of the scriptural texts Paul cites, his argument at various points seems tenuous. Deuteronomy, after all, is not concerned to drive a wedge between faith and law; it is the book that includes the call to Israel to hear that the LORD is one, to love the LORD with all one's being,

and on that basis to keep and teach the words of his command
(6:4–9). Indeed, Jesus cited that passage, known as the *Shema
Yisrael* (the "Hear, O Israel"), as the principal point of the law
(see Mark 12:29–30). And the promise to the "seed" in Genesis does not seem to be messianic in the original text or in
the Septuagint;[10] the term appears to be a collective reference
to Abraham's progeny and is translated "descendants" in the
Revised Standard Version.

But Paul's interpretation does not stand or fall by modern standards of exegesis. His use of Scripture is instrumental
because his point is more theological than exegetical:

> For you are all sons of God through faith in Christ Jesus.
> For as many as were baptized into Christ, were clothed in
> Christ. There is neither Jew nor Greek, neither slave nor
> free, neither male nor female: for you are all one in Christ
> Jesus. And if you are of Christ, then you are Abraham's
> seed, heirs according to promise. (Gal. 3:26–29)

Once that is understood to be the central theme of Scripture, realized whenever one appropriates one's new identity
in baptism, it becomes the point of interpretation to illustrate
the theme.

For all that the documents of Israel's canon may vary, for all
that their periods and perspectives differ, the documents attest
a single truth on Paul's reading. What is said in the case of
Abraham amounts to "the Scripture foreseeing that God would
make the Gentiles righteous by faith" (Gal. 3:8). "Scripture"
for Paul is what the documents finally mean, the ultimate significance in the light of which the interpretation of individual
documents and passages unfolds. That is why it is natural for
Paul to proceed from Christ to the passages at issue: the point
of departure was the point at which one had arrived by means
of baptism.

---

10. Paul may have been influenced by the interpretation of some of the
Aramaic Targumim at this point. Even so, he would have known that the
Septuagint did not engage in such a messianic reading.

James's Interpretation of David

The confrontation at Antioch that Paul recounts to his audience in Galatia did not turn out happily for him at the time. His explanation of his own point of view is triumphant and ringing only in retrospect. Indeed, by the time he recollects his argument for the benefit of the Galatians, he seems so confident that one might overlook the fact that he was the loser in the battle with the representatives of James. But as he says himself, Peter, Barnabas, and "the rest of the Jews" declined fellowship at meals with Gentiles (Gal. 2:11–13).

The position of James is not represented, as is Paul's, by a writing of James himself.[11] But the book of Acts does clearly reflect his perspective in regard to both circumcision and the issue of purity (Acts 15), the two principal matters of concern in Galatians. The account in Acts 15 is romanticized; one sees much less tension and controversy than in Paul's account. But once allowance has been made for the tendency in Acts to portray the ancient Church as a body in harmonious unity, the nature and force of James's position become clear.

The two issues in dispute, circumcision and purity, are dealt with in Acts 15 as if they were the agenda of a single meeting of leaders in Jerusalem. (Paul in Galatians 2 more accurately describes the meeting he had with the leaders as distinct from a later decision to return to the question of purity.) The first item on the agenda is settled by having Peter declare that, since God gave his holy spirit to Gentiles who believed, no attempt should be made to add requirements such as circumcision to burden them (Acts 15:6–11). Paul could scarcely have said it better himself.[12]

The second item on the agenda is settled on James's authority, not Peter's, and the outcome is not in line with Paul's thought. James first confirms the position of Peter, but he states

---

11. The letter attributed to James in the New Testament is pseudepigraphic. The work of Martin Dibelius, recently updated, is still basic; see *Der Brief des Jakobus* (Göttingen: Vandenhoeck und Ruprecht, 1984).

12. Acts often portrays the apostles generally as sharing Paul's position (and his vocabulary). The overall perspective of the document is a development of Pauline theology.

the position in a very different way: "Symeon[13] has related how God first visited the Gentiles, to take a people in his name" (Acts 15:14). James's perspective here is not that all who believe are Israel (the Pauline definition) but that *in addition* to Israel God has established a people in his name. How the new people are to be regarded in relation to Israel is a question that is implicit in the statement, and James goes on to answer it.

James develops the relationship between those taken from the Gentiles and Israel in two ways. The first method is the use of Scripture, while the second is a requirement of purity. The logic of them both inevitably involves a rejection of Paul's position (along the lines laid out in Galatians 2).

The use of Scripture, like the argument itself, is quite unlike Paul's. James claims that "with this [that is, his statement of Peter's position] the words of the prophets agree, just as it is written" (Acts 15:15), and he goes on to cite from the book of Amos. (The passage cited will concern us in a moment.)

The form of James's interpretation is an immediate indication of a substantial difference from Paul. As James has it, there is actual agreement between Symeon and the words of the prophets, as two people might agree.[14] The continuity of Christian experience with Scripture is marked as a greater concern than within Paul's interpretation, and James expects that continuity to be verbal, a matter of agreement with the prophets' words, not merely with possible ways of looking at what they mean.

The citation from Amos (9:11–12)[15] comports well with James's concern that the position of the Church agree with the principal vocabulary of the prophets:

> After this I will come back and restore the tent of David which has fallen, and rebuild its ruins and set it up anew, that the rest of men may seek the LORD, and all the Gentiles upon whom my name is called. (Acts 15:16–17)

---

13. The Semitic form of Peter's name, which is usually given as "Simon," following the Greek spelling.

14. The verb in question is *symphōnéō*, which is only used at this point in the New Testament to speak of agreement with Scripture. Usually, the term refers to the concord of people in conversation.

15. The citation is in the form of the Septuagint, in keeping with the usual policy in the book of Acts.

In the argument of James as represented here, what the belief of Gentiles achieves is not the redefinition of Israel (as in Paul's thought) but the restoration of the house of David. The argument is possible because a Davidic genealogy of Jesus (and his brother James) is assumed.

An account of James's preaching in the Temple is given by Hegesippus, who wrote during the second century.[16] James there represents Jesus as the Son of Man who is to come from heaven to judge the world.[17] Those who agree cry out, "Hosanna to the son of David!" Hegesippus shows that James's view of his brother came to be that he was related to David (as was the family generally) and was also a heavenly figure who was coming to judge the world.[18]

Acts and Hegesippus together show James contending that Jesus restored the house of David because he was the agent of final judgment and was being accepted as such by Gentiles.

But on James's view, Gentiles remain Gentiles; they are not to be identified with Israel. His position was not anti-Pauline, at least not at first. His focus was on Jesus' role as the ultimate arbiter within the Davidic line, and there was never any question in his mind: the Temple was the natural place to worship God and acknowledge Jesus.[19] Embracing the Temple as central meant for James, as it meant for everyone associated with worship there, maintaining the purity that it was understood that God required in his house. Purity involved excluding Gentiles from the interior courts of the Temple, where Israel was involved in sacrifice. The line of demarcation between Israel and non-Israel was no invention within the circle of James but a natural result of seeing Jesus as the triumphant scion of the house of David.

In James's understanding, gentile belief in Jesus was there-

---

16. His work is cited in Eusebius, *Ecclesiastical History* 2.23, a fourth-century work.

17. The imagery is inspired by Dan. 7:13–14, where "Son of Man" is used to refer to an angelic figure in God's heavenly court.

18. The resurrection was the catalyst that prompted his thinking. Prior to that, there was conflict between Jesus and James (as between Jesus and his brothers generally); see Mark 3:31–34 and John 7:2–9.

19. Hegesippus goes to great length to describe James's punctilious devotion to the Temple.

fore a vindication of his Davidic triumph, but it did not involve a fundamental change in the status of Gentiles vis-à-vis Israel. This characterization of the Gentiles, developed by means of the reference to Amos, enables James to proceed to his requirement that Gentiles recognize the need for purity. He first states that "I determine not to trouble those of the Gentiles who turn to God" (Acts 15:19), as if he were simply repeating the policy of Peter in regard to circumcision. (The implicit authority of that "I" contrasts sharply with the usual portrayal in Acts of apostolic decision as communal.) But he then continues that his determination is also "to write to them to abstain from the pollutions of the idols, and from fornication, and from what is strangled, and from blood" (Acts 15:20).

The rules set out by James are designed to separate believing Gentiles from their ambient cultural environment. They are to refrain from feasts in honor of the gods and from foods sacrificed to idols in the course of being butchered and sold. (The notional devotion of animals in the market to one god or another was a common practice in the Hellenistic world.) They are to observe stricter limits than usual on the type of sexual activity they might engage in, and with whom. They are to avoid the flesh of animals that have been strangled instead of bled, and they are not to consume blood itself. The proscription of blood, of course, was basic within Judaism (see Lev. 7:27; Deut. 12:16). And strangling an animal (as distinct from cutting its throat) increased the availability of blood in the meat. Such strictures are consistent with James's initial observation, that God had taken a people from the Gentiles (15:14); they were to be similar to Israel in their distinction from the Hellenistic world at large.

The motive behind the rules is not separation in itself, however. James links them to the fact that the Mosaic legislation regarding purity is well and widely known: "For Moses from early generations has had those preaching him city by city, being read in the synagogues every sabbath" (Acts 15:21). Because the law is well known, James insists that believers, even gentile believers, are not to live in flagrant violation of it. As a result of James's insistence, the meeting in Jerusalem decides to send envoys and a letter to Antioch, in order to require Gentiles to honor the prohibitions set out by James (Acts 15:22–35).

The same chapter of Leviticus that commands "Love your neighbor as yourself" (19:18) also forbids blood to be eaten (19:26) and fornication (19:29; see also 18:6–30). The canonical (but secondhand) Letter of James calls the commandment of love "the royal law" (James 2:8),[20] acknowledging that Jesus had accorded it privilege by citing it alongside the commandment to love God as the two greatest commandments (see Mark 12:28–34). In Acts, James himself, while accepting that Gentiles cannot be required to keep the whole law, insists that they should acknowledge it by observing basic requirements concerning fornication and blood.

It is of interest that Leviticus forbids the eating of blood by sojourners as well as Israelites and associates that prohibition with how animals are to be killed for the purpose of eating (17:10–16). Moreover, a principle of exclusivity in sacrifice is trenchantly maintained: anyone, whether of Israel or a sojourner dwelling among them, who offers a sacrifice that is not brought to the LORD's honor in the Temple is to be cut off from the people (17:8–9). In other words, the prohibitions of James, involving sacrifice, fornication, strangled meat produce, and blood, all derive easily from the very context in Leviticus from which the commandment to love comes. They are elementary and involve interest in what Gentiles as well as Israelites do.[21]

James's prohibitions are designed to show that believing Gentiles honor the law, which is commonly read, without in any way changing their status as Gentiles. Thereby, the tent of David is erected again, this time in the midst of Gentiles who show their awareness of the restoration by respecting the Torah. The interpretation attributed to James involves an application of Davidic vocabulary to Jesus, as is consistent with the claim of Jesus' family to Davidic ancestry.[22] The transfer of Davidic promises to Jesus is accomplished within an acceptance

---

20. The letter is generally regarded as a highly derivative version of James's position, which was composed well after Paul's position became well known, around 90 C.E.

21. At a later period, the Talmud would also see the formulation of "Noachic commandments," which Gentiles were to keep. See Sanh. 56B.

22. In contrast, Paul considered Jesus' descent from David as "according to the flesh" (Rom. 1:3); he did not cite it as a demonstration of divine authority.

of the terms of reference of the Scripture generally: to embrace David is to embrace Moses. James's interpretation harbors no trace of the Pauline gambit, which sets one biblical principle (justification in the manner of Abraham) against another (obedience in the manner of Moses).[23] Where Paul divided the Scripture against itself in order to maintain the integrity of a single fellowship of Jews and Gentiles, James insisted upon the integrity of Scripture, even at the cost of separating Christians from one another. In both cases, the interpretation of Scripture was also — at the same moment as the sacred text was apprehended — a matter of social policy.

Peter's Interpretation of Moses

Of all the disputants in the controversy at Antioch, Peter comes off the worst in Paul's account in Galatians 2. Not only is he said to go along with Paul, only then to side with James in separating from Gentiles (Gal. 2:11–13), but Paul claims to have taken the occasion to deliver a diatribe on faith and works, using Peter's "hypocrisy" as his point of departure (Gal. 2:14–21). Indeed, it is difficult to see, on Paul's accounting, why Paul ever left Antioch, which is just what Acts says that he did some time after the envoys of James had visited (Acts 15:36–41).

Peter's position in the dispute is difficult to characterize because Paul makes a caricature of it, and Acts virtually ignores it in favor of depicting James as the operative authority. But Peter is definitely associated in the New Testament with a style of interpretation that is distinct from Paul's and James's. It is a style of great nuance and resonance, but without the unequivocal finding of a Pauline new Israel or a Jacobean scion of David. Peter appears to have worked more in comparative terms than in an effort to legislate by interpretation.

In the absence of direct evidence of the Petrine use of Scripture,[24] the best source for an example is the material in the

---

23. At a later period, the Letter of James would dispute any such reading with the statement, "Show me your faith apart from your works, and I by my works will show you my faith" (2:18).

24. Both 1 Peter and 2 Peter are examples of writings from a later period (no

Gospels attributed to Peter. From the second century, scholars of the Church pointed to Mark's Gospel especially as an interpretation of the teaching of Peter.[25] Peter in Mark appears frequently as the representative of the apostles, often in association with James and John, the sons of Zebedee. In one such passage, the influence of the Hebrew Bible is palpable.

In Mark 9:2–8, Jesus takes Peter, James, and John up a high mountain, and he is transformed before them. His clothing shines white; Moses and Elijah appear, speaking with him. Peter offers to make three booths, one for Jesus, one for Moses, and one for Elijah, but a cloud covers the scene, and a voice from the cloud says, "This is my beloved son, hear him." When the apostles are able to see again, only Jesus is there.

The reference to Moses and Elijah makes it plain that the Transfiguration requires an understanding of the Hebrew Bible in order to be understood. Both of those prophetic figures were associated with revelation upon a mountain. Moses' mountain is called both Sinai and Horeb in the Pentateuch, following the designations of distinct, traditional sources. Elijah is placed on Horeb by the same tradition that knows Moses' mountain under that name (1 Kings 19).

But the Transfiguration resonates with a particular scene in the Pentateuch. In Exodus 24, Moses takes three followers with him up the mountain, as the particular representatives of an elite group (of seventy elders). Before they go up the mountain, Moses orders the preparation of a sacrifice at which the people as a whole accept the words of the LORD given to Moses as the covenant between them and the LORD (Exod. 24:3–8). Then comes the ascent of the mountain and a vision of God (24:9–11). Moses is invited to ascend further, and a cloud of glory covers the mountain;[26] on the seventh day the LORD calls to him, so that he can receive the tables of stone over the next forty days (Exod. 24:12–18).

---

earlier than 90 C.E.) that attempt to apply the Petrine approach to situations that arose well after Peter's death. A widely accepted tradition has him perish in Rome during the persecution of Nero in 64 C.E.

25. The first and most important witness is Papias, whose tradition is quoted in Eusebius's *Ecclesiastical History* (3.39.15).

26. "Glory," of course, is understood to shine, as does Moses' face when he returns from Mount Sinai (Exod. 34:29–35).

The narrative structure of the Transfiguration is identical to Moses' ascent of Sinai: the motifs of a single master, three disciples from a wider group, the sacred mountain, the cloud, the vision, the voice, are all shared. Just as the LORD called to Moses on the seventh day (Exod. 24:16), so Jesus took his three followers up his mountain "after six days" (Mark 9:2). The connection between the two passages is evident, but what does that connection suggest?

Although the focus of the Transfiguration is on Jesus in his divinely disclosed identity as God's son, the identification is worked out within the general terms of reference to Moses and Elijah and by means of particular motifs of the solemnization of the covenant in Exodus 24. The Transfiguration is so wedded to Scripture as the substance of what is revealed, it is difficult to draw the line between experience and interpretation. But that is exactly the point of the Transfiguration: neither experience alone nor interpretation alone will attest the truth of Jesus' identity. But together they furnish a vision of who precisely he is.

The vision of Jesus may be mediated to anyone who attends to the Transfiguration within its scriptural terms of reference. An allusion to the Transfiguration in 2 Peter (1:16–21) is instructive. There, the vision is held to be the basis on which Peter made known the power of Jesus Christ, but then the passage goes on to say, "And we have more certain the prophetic word" (2 Pet. 1:19). That is, once Jesus is correctly seen in prophetic terms, Scripture's prophecy finds its purpose, and whoever knows Scripture in that sense has access to the divine spirit of prophecy (2 Pet. 1:20, 21). Both interpretation and experience are merely means to an end: the possession of spirit.

Finally, the Petrine approach to Scripture neither makes Moses subservient to Jesus (the Pauline approach) nor makes Jesus subservient to Moses (the Jacobean approach). Although Peter's account of the Transfiguration is not conceptually sophisticated, it is elegant: the prophetic covenant of Moses and the divine sonship of Jesus stand side by side, such that the one interprets the other. Of course, such a delicate balancing of two principles is problematic as an engine of social policy among believers: Who can say in a given case whether the spirit of prophecy behind the Scripture agrees more with what the text says or with what one experiences in the community of Jesus?

According to Acts 15, Peter concluded on the basis of God's gift of the spirit to Gentiles that they could not be required to be circumcised (Acts 15:6–11). On the other hand, Paul shows in Galatians 2 that Peter was not willing to make a general principle for or against Mosaic requirements and that he could change his mind when confronted with differing interpretations and practices. But his apparent ambivalence reflects a commitment to his twin loyalties to a single son and a single law, together mediating the same spirit.

Conclusion

The three most influential approaches to Scripture within primitive Christianity were not simply theories of interpretation. Each came from within formative circles of the Church, and each was involved in how communities were ordered. Each was implicated in the preparation of catechumens for baptism within the traditions of a given circle. And each has left an indelible impression upon the character of the Church.

The Pauline approach is the most directly and fulsomely attested in the New Testament. Not only Paul's own letters, but writings from a later period in his name and style, as well as Acts, represent the deep influence of a genuinely radical intellectual. Paul's claim that baptism made for a new Israel, after the manner of Abraham but no longer subject to the Mosaic law, was in his own time a closely argued but controversial position. Only the growing number of gentile believers, as well as the destruction of the Temple and its consequences, would permit Pauline Christianity to become representative of the movement as a whole.

Once the tide of change moved in his favor, Paul arguably became the most influential intellectual in the history of the West. Paul's theology challenges any appeal to normative law within the social order of the Church. This has been difficult for many Christians to accept. The Reformation was — among other things — an attempt to assert that Pauline the-

ology, rather than any law, was normative within the Church.
The factionalism that ensued — between Roman Catholics and
Protestants, and *among* Protestants — is still characteristic of
Christian experience.

Just as Paul's influence grew unpredictably, James's declined
precipitately from the time of the destruction of the Temple.
The natural center of the movement in Jerusalem was given
up to places such as Alexandria, Antioch, Corinth, Damascus, Ephesus, and Rome. The force of a genuinely Christian
Judaism, extended to Gentiles insofar as they would embrace
some form of Jewish Christianity, was certainly felt long after
James was martyred. But demography, as well as history, was
against his clear definition of the movement in unequivocally
Mosaic terms.

In the stark contrast between Paul and James, Peter can seem
an artless compromiser, agreeing now with one, now with another. But the twin emphases of Peter upon Scripture and Jesus
together, as providing the insight of the spirit, would prove to
be a dominant influence in the formation of the Gospels. At the
same time, the often unpredictable policy of early Christianity,
sometimes siding with the traditions of Israel, sometimes with
the new practices of believing communities, is explicable more
easily on the basis of a Petrine approach than on the basis of a
Pauline or a Jacobean approach.

Christians have typically believed that their inspiration
comes both from Scripture and from their faithful practice
and that the single spirit — the spirit of God — unites them
both. This emphasis upon a purely theological consistency,
even at the expense of inevitable conflict in the social realm,
is an inheritance of Petrine teaching. Any attempt to judge
Christianity on the basis of social consistency alone will result in disappointment and confusion. The Church inevitably
appears insufficiently radical or insufficiently conservative to
secular historians, depending upon their bent. That is because
its identity lies in the dialectic between Scripture and practice,
tradition and experience, a dialectic that it knows under the
name of the spirit of God.

Once the distinctive character of each of the three major approaches is appreciated, the appearance of conflict in the early

Church becomes easily understood. At the same time, the christological focus of all three approaches is evident. Of course, it may seem obvious to say that Christian interpretation found Christ at the center of the meaning of Scripture. But none of the founding interpreters involved — not James, not Paul, not Peter — set out from the beginning to create a religion different from Judaism. The question therefore emerges: Why did they resemble one another in christological terms? What is the common denominator that gives them their family resemblance? This is the leading question to be addressed in the next chapter. Once it has been dealt with, we may then turn to the issue of how the three approaches to Scripture coalesced in the New Testament.

5

Jesus: The Genesis of Christian Interpretation

The christological reading of Scripture, in the circles of James, Paul, and Peter, was a characteristic of early Christian interpretation. Two foci — the text and the significance of Jesus — are clearly present within each of these major streams of interpretative approach. James's foci are the most easily defined: they are (1) Scripture, and (2) the Davidic scion who fulfills the promises God made to Israel. Paul's foci required more explanation in his own time, but they can be understood as (1) Scripture, and (2) the Israel created by faith in Jesus Christ. Finally, the Petrine circle found its foci in (1) Scripture, and (2) the shared authority of Jesus and Moses.

The pattern of two foci, of an overarching principle alongside Scripture within the act of interpretation, is shared among various sorts of Judaic and Christian exegesis. There is, of course, no sense in which Christian interpretation may be distinguished from others as being "creative," as if Judaic readings were simply a matter of stating the plain meaning of texts. The belief that a text has a single, circumstantial meaning is a recent development (since the Enlightenment) and has been severely challenged by postmodernism. (For that reason, postmodern critics have given more attention to ancient interpreters than was the habit among Enlightenment and modern critics.) Judaic readings of Scripture quite typically explored a range of meaning alongside the immediate sense of the text concerned. The result could be daring, complex, and rich in symbolism.

What distinguished Christian from Judaic interpretation,

then, was not the fact that it was possessed of two foci. At Qumran, the covenanters (attached to the Essene movement generally) developed a type of exegesis called the *Pesher*. In the various *Pesherim*, biblical works are cited passage by passage and related to the recent history of the Essenes, their present position, and their final triumph as the sons of light against the sons of darkness. The covenanters read Scripture as the enciphered counsel of God. Their technique of the *Pesher* is related to apocalyptic literature generally, where symbols were used and texts interpreted in order to predict the cataclysmic end of history in the triumph of God.[1]

A more famous type of Judaic exegesis is midrash, where the meanings found in Scripture can be as esoteric as any found in a text from Qumran. Midrash, as several commentators on the New Testament have pointed out, comes from the verb *darash*, "to search out." In that Christian interpreters "searched out" a meaning, their christological exegesis is sometimes called "midrash." But midrash proper is in fact the product of rabbis who worked for a specific purpose: to relate the Torah taught on the authority of their predecessors to the Torah revealed to Moses on Sinai. A single Israel was, in the rabbinic understanding, a function of what came to be seen as two revelations of the Torah, in writing and in the academy. That typical focus on the Torah, written and oral, as well as on a given text of Scripture, is what essentially distinguished midrash from other sorts of interpretation and what makes direct comparison with the interpretation of Scripture found in the New Testament inappropriate.

Not all Judaic exegesis was conducted in Aramaic or Hebrew. Works such as the Wisdom of Solomon (from the Apocrypha) illustrate how the ideas as well as the language of Greek philosophy were appropriated within the interpretation of Scripture. "Wisdom" for many Jews was not simply an attribute of God but a vibrant and accessible personality; conceived of as a woman, she is the friend of sages and an intimate of God in

---

1. The element of prediction, often to the point of providing a calendar of the last things, is what distinguishes apocalyptic literature within eschatological thought more generally.

creation at one and the same time (Wisdom of Solomon 8). Wisdom was seen so persistently within the text of Scripture by some interpreters, such as Philo of Alexandria, that it is difficult to tell whether the purpose of the exercise is exegesis or philosophy. In fact, it is both; the disciples of Wisdom saw her as clearly in the text as the rabbis saw Torah and the Essenes saw the resolution of history in their favor.

The Kingdom of God
as Jesus' Interpretative Principle

No person who has read the relevant sources attentively will deny that Jesus' preaching of the kingdom of God was rooted in the conception of the kingdom within early Judaism. That has been a matter of consensus since the end of the nineteenth century. The discovery of the importance of early Judaic theology as the foundation and milieu of Jesus' theology was nothing short of revolutionary in its impact.[2]

What most of all struck scholars at the end of the last century was that "the kingdom of God" within early Judaism was a reference neither to an individual's life after death in heaven nor to a movement of social improvement upon the earth. Those had been dominant understandings, deeply embedded in the theology and preaching of the late nineteenth century, prior to the brilliant and incontrovertible assertions of Johannes Weiss and Albert Schweitzer. These scholars demonstrated that the kingdom of God in early Judaism and the preaching of Jesus referred to God's final judgment of the world; the concept was part and parcel of the anticipation of the last things (*eskhata* in Greek, from which the term "eschatology" comes).

Christian thought has been in some confusion ever since Weiss and Schweitzer made their point. Some scholars attempt to deny that Jesus' teaching was eschatological, although it is difficult to see how Jesus' promise of a coming feast with

---

2. For a detailed consideration, see Bruce Chilton, *The Kingdom of God in the Teaching of Jesus* (London: SPCK; Philadelphia: Fortress, 1984); and idem, "The Kingdom of God in Recent Discussion," in *Studying the Historical Jesus*, ed. Bruce Chilton and C. A. Evans (Leiden: Brill, 1994).

Abraham, Isaac, and Jacob (see Matt. 8:11; Luke 13:28–29), for instance, is anything other than a reference to a future definitively changed by God. On the other hand, the awareness that Jesus referred to the future has caused some scholars to focus exclusively upon the issue of eschatology, as if Jesus' whole purpose were to provide an eschatological calendar (in the manner of apocalyptic literature). A kind of middle ground has been staked out by those who accept that Jesus' thought was indeed eschatological but who then try to find a way around the difficulty that the world has continued on its less than cheerful way for some two millennia since it was supposed to be near ending. What sort of messiah can have been so mistaken? Scholars of the middle ground tend to argue that Jesus spoke of the end of things in order to dramatize his own claim to authority.

None of the three approaches is entirely satisfactory. To deny the eschatology of Jesus is simply to eliminate from consideration a substantial element of what the New Testament says he taught. What is inconvenient for modern purposes should not be wished away from ancient sources. But to focus exclusively upon Jesus' eschatology makes him appear to be an apocalyptist in the manner of the book of Daniel, although none of the Gospels can be called an apocalyptic work. Moreover, if Jesus preached a single calendar of the last things, it is difficult to explain the variety of apocalyptic expectations in the movement that he founded. Finally, to argue that his eschatology was a cipher for his own authority ignores the emphasis in Jesus' preaching on the kingdom itself, rather than his personal identity. The argument also leaves us with the anomaly that a conception of time that proves faulty is a curious advertisement for the authority of Jesus' teaching.

Once the challenge of eschatology has been appreciated, it is easy to understand why much Christian thought has been in a retreat from its own Scriptures for most of the twentieth century. "Liberals" have attempted to replace the kingdom with a social gospel rooted in hopes for progress in the world as a natural and human system. "Conservatives" have attempted to replace the message of the kingdom with the insistence that the messenger himself is divine. Scholarly discussion of the kingdom in Jesus' preaching, meanwhile, has often been reduced to an unproductive debate between those who characterize it as eschatological and those who refuse to do so.

What has not been sufficiently recognized is that the notion of the kingdom of God was deeply embedded in the language of early Judaism and was a means of expressing God's activity in the world. It misses the point to consider only what is possible within the world, or only the divine source of the kingdom's influence. To say that God is active in the world implies that the world as we know it is changing. To speak of the kingdom denies the truism that nothing changes in this world and the truism that God is best known as an immutable power beyond our realm. The point of speaking of God's kingdom is that he makes his realm ours. The book of Psalms refers distinctly to God's activity as king, and eschatology appears as one dimension of his activity, because the future is the natural climax in any assertion that God is making this world his. But alongside the eschatological dimension in Psalms, there are four other dimensions of God's royal activity, as well.

In order to facilitate consideration, the five emphatic dimensions of the kingdom of God will be cited here and illustrated by means of key passages from the book of Psalms.[3] In the Psalms we must reckon with a much more nuanced application of a language of kingship to God than the modern fixation upon eschatology would allow. The assertion that God is king refers normally to his rule on behalf of his people: (1) as present and to come; (2) as intervening and becoming all-pervasive; (3) as demanding righteousness and anticipating perfection; (4) as requiring a purity commensurate with God's sanctity; (5) and as extending from Israel so as to be inclusive of all peoples.

Five dimensions of the kingdom, then, play a paradigmatic role within the book of Psalms:

1. The eschatological dimension — the kingdom is so near in time as to be present, and yet ultimate from the point of view of full disclosure:

---

3. The book of Psalms is here used as a basis of discussion because it was familiar from the usage of various psalms in the Temple and was deeply influential in the development of later conceptions of the kingdom.

> Say among the nations that the LORD reigns.
> The world is established, so as not to move;
> he shall judge the peoples with equity. (96:10)

2. The dimension of transcendence — the kingdom is forceful in its impact but will permeate all things:

> All your creatures will give you thanks, LORD,
> and your faithful will bless you;
> they shall speak of the glory of your kingdom,
> and tell of your might,
> to make your mighty deeds known to the sons of men,
> and the glorious splendor of his kingdom. (145:10–12)

3. The dimension of judgment — the kingdom is ever righteous but attains to consummation:

> Break the arm of the wicked, and evil;
> search out his wickedness until it cannot be found!
> The LORD is king for ever and ever;
> the nations perish from his earth! (10:15–16)

4. The dimension of purity — the kingdom is consistent only with what is clean, until all things are holy (relevant here in view of the reference to God as king in vv. 7–10):

> Who will ascend the mount of the LORD,
> and who will stand in his holy place?
> The innocent of hands and pure of heart,
> who has not lifted up his soul to vanity,
> and has not sworn deceitfully. (24:3–4)

5. The dimension of radiation — although the kingdom is local (in Zion and in heaven), it is to include all peoples, even uniting Israel and the nations:

> God reigns over the nations;
> God sits upon his holy throne.
> The nobles of the peoples are gathered, the people of
> the God of Abraham;
> for the shields of the earth are God's. He is highly
> exalted! (47:8–9)

The five dimensions are so closely related within the language of the kingdom, one example from the Psalms might be used to illustrate more than one aspect.[4] That tends to confirm that we have here identified basic dimensions of meaning for the kingdom. A given speaker or circle of usage would of course develop a particular significance, appropriate to the historical conditions involved (during the time of Psalms, or later).

Within each dimension, the first pole designates the kingdom as it impinges upon those who might respond to it; for them, the kingdom appears as (1) near; (2) powerful; (3) demanding; (4) pure; and (5) associated with Zion in particular. The second pole of each dimension designates the goal implicit within the kingdom, the (1) final; (2) immanent; (3) faultless; (4) holy; and (5) inclusive reality it promises to be. The kingdom of God, in other words, is a scandal for modern thinking because it purports to be final. It is indeed eschatological in respect of time, as Weiss and Schweitzer maintained, but also transcendent in respect of place (in Zion, heaven, everywhere), perfect in respect of action, sacred in its purity, and all-embracing in its choice of Israel.

Jesus' gospel of the kingdom represented a distinctive development of dimensions of usage that had already been established for the meaning of God's kingdom. Perhaps his most signal innovation was the very act of announcing the kingdom: what was generally known as a promise of the Scripture was claimed by Jesus to be available to the people he addressed in disparate towns and villages in Galilee.

The particular form of words that he used, "kingdom of God," came from his Aramaic-speaking milieu. The phrase is well attested in the Targums — Aramaic paraphrases of the Hebrew Bible. Repeatedly, when the Hebrew text refers to God acting on behalf of his people, the Prophetic Targums sometimes read "kingdom of God" or "kingdom of the LORD."[5] The personal nature of kingdom (as God himself) was emphasized

---

4. When the wider context of each passage is considered, the observation is all the more valid.

5. Key passages are analyzed in detail in Bruce Chilton, *A Galilean Rabbi and His Bible* (Wilmington, Del.: Glazier; London: SPCK, 1984), 57–60.

by Jesus when he compared the kingdom in his parables to kings and to other persons.

To promulgate the kingdom as a message was to claim God's forceful intervention in its classic dimensions, along the lines of time, place, actions, objects, and people. Those dimensions in fact become explicit in Jesus' preaching in a saying already mentioned, one usually said to come from the source of Jesus' sayings called "Q":[6]

> Many shall come from east and west
> and recline in feasting
> with Abraham and Isaac and Jacob.
>   (Matt. 8:11; Luke 13:28, 29)

There can be no doubt of the emphasis upon a future consummation in the saying, involving a particular (but unnamed) place, the actions and material of festivity (including the luxurious custom of reclining, not sitting, at a banquet), and the incorporation of the many who shall rejoice in the company of the patriarchs.

Jesus' use of the imagery of feasting in order to refer to the kingdom, a characteristic of his message, is resonant both with early Judaic language of the kingdom and with his own ministry. The picture of God offering a feast on Mount Zion "for all peoples," where death itself is swallowed up, becomes an influential image from the time of Isa. 25:6–8. Notably, the Targum of Isaiah refers to the divine disclosure on Mount Zion that includes the image of the feast as "the kingdom of the LORD of hosts" (24:23).[7] Sayings such as the one cited from "Q" invoke that imagery, and Jesus' practice of fellowship at meals with his disciples and many others amounted to a claim that the ultimate festivity had already begun.

The dynamic of inclusion is not without its dark side, both in Isaiah and in Jesus' preaching. The Isaian feast on Mount Zion

---

6. For a detailed analysis of the saying, see Bruce Chilton, *God in Strength: Jesus' Announcement of the Kingdom* (Sheffield, England: Sheffield Academic Press, 1987), reprinted from the series Studien zum Neuen Testament und seiner Umwelt (Freistadt: Plöchl, 1979), 179–201. The significant differences between Matthew and Luke here show that Q was not the stable source some scholars claim it was.

7. See the discussion in Chilton, *Galilean Rabbi*, 57–63.

is to be accompanied by the destruction of Moab (25:10–12);[8] in Jesus' saying, the feast with the patriarchs includes the threat of exclusion for some (Matt. 8:12; Luke 13:28). The ethics of the imagery, which at first may seem to involve little more than an ethos of festivity, turn out to imply the dimension of judgment, as is natural within an expectation of the kingdom.

The kingdom of God in the saying from "Q" is a feast for the future whose invitation is issued now by Jesus, so that response to the invitation is implicitly a condition of entry. The feast's location is implicitly related to Mount Zion, where Isaiah predicted a feast for all peoples. The judgment of the kingdom will exclude the wicked, and what is enjoyed in luxurious fashion will be pure. Finally, the kingdom's radiant power will include those from far away, all of whom are to be joined with the patriarchs. No wonder Jesus himself had to face the question, among those who responded to his gospel, What is the way into this kingdom?

The image of a feast that appears in Matt. 8:11, 12; Luke 13:28, 29 is developed along narrative lines in what is commonly known as the parable of the wedding feast, after the version in Matt. 22:1–10 (cf. Luke 14:16–24). Within the parable, Jesus engages in the rabbinic method of using narrative in order to recommend a certain ethical performance.[9] The feast is prepared, but invitations must be accepted in order to be effective, and God is ready to drag outsiders in, rather than permit the festivity to go unattended. Within the festal imagery we have just considered, the parable is an interesting development. Who would conceive of the Isaian feast being passed up by those invited? The Jesus of this tradition, however, conceives of the kingdom as elusive; the invited are willfully ignorant of it. The parable's narrative, that is to say, conveys the kingdom within a fresh perspective. The narrative is designed as performance, to speak without words of what the kingdom means for us.

---

8. In the Targum, "Moab" is used as a symbol to identify the oppressor of Israel as Rome, and the reference is distributed through the chapter; see Bruce Chilton, *The Isaiah Targum: Introduction, Translation, Apparatus, and Notes,* The Aramaic Bible (Wilmington, Del.: Glazier; Edinburgh: T & T Clark, 1987), 47–51.

9. See Bruce Chilton and J. T. McDonald, *Jesus and the Ethics of the Kingdom* (Grand Rapids: Eerdmans; London: SPCK, 1987), 31–37.

The performance of meaning effected by the parable is not entirely a matter of reference to the imaginary. Precisely because the parable concerns God's activity as king, it makes a claim within the experience of anyone who knows what a king is. God, the parable claims, has been brought to act as a sovereign in a surprising way. His present offer is out of the ordinary. The extraordinarily bad, even violent, behavior of those who should have been guests provides the impetus for a radical expansion in scope of an increasingly insistent invitation: leave your cares, however legitimate, and join the feast; accept this invitation you could never have anticipated. The parabolic motif portrays divine activity as begun but not as perfected. The parabolic actions point toward the future as the locus of the kingdom's ultimate disclosure. Similarly, the ethical theme of the parable frames and encourages a wary, clever — even opportunistic — response to the disclosure that is under way but not complete.

Although the kingdom of God is a theme that Jesus derived from the biblical tradition (in Targumic form), it obviously acquired a life of its own within his teaching. He did not limit his reference to passages of Scripture with which the theme was associated; he did not even require a scriptural occasion in order to invoke the idea. He thought it could be known by means of his narrative parables, as well as within the world of Scripture. There is ample precedent among the rabbis for the notion that a narrative parable might disclose the way in which God is or will be king;[10] Jesus' distinctiveness lies in the way in which the theme of the kingdom is consistently at the focus of his concern.

The parables of growth are unusual in literary terms since there do not seem to be precise analogies within rabbinic literature. They underscore the extent to which Jesus held that the kingdom is a matter of experience, something one might participate in by observation. Acuity is demanded because growth is not something Jesus takes for granted. In the parable of the man, the seed, and the earth, it is stressed that the farmer has no idea how the crop is produced but that he wields his sickle at the right time nonetheless (Mark 4:26–29). Mustard seed be-

---

10. See ibid.

comes a "tree" (so Matt. 13:31–32 and Luke 13:18–19) or makes "big branches" (Mark 4:30–32) without an interval of time being indicated; the emphasis is on beginning and result, rather than process.[11] These parables are told as a lens of the kingdom, so that the hearer might see how the kingdom of God reveals itself.

Growth as understood by Jesus has the same dimensions as the kingdom. It is aimed at the future and intervenes as miracle on the way to spreading itself abroad; it demands specific behavior and takes place only on pure ground; its natural extension leads to greater and greater inclusion. As the principle of Scripture, the kingdom's growth effectively transcends Scripture in Jesus' teaching.·

The extent to which Scripture for Jesus illustrated a larger theme is reflected in the quotations of texts attributed to him in the Gospels. Repeatedly, Jesus cites texts only briefly, sometimes in a fractured form. For example, he warns hearers to avoid behavior that will get them cast into "Gehenna, where their worm does not die and the fire is not quenched" (Mark 9:47–48).[12] The phrasing comes from the last verse of the book of Isaiah (66:24), and the connection with Gehenna, the place of eschatological punishment, is explicitly made in the Targum of Isaiah. But the wording does not exactly correspond to any known version of Isaiah. The idea of Gehenna with its Targumic imagery is invoked in order to warn of the consequences of duplicity: better to remove an eye or spindle a text than to lose the focus on the kingdom.

Jesus' use of Scripture is radically instrumental because his other focus, alongside the text, is truly his principal focus. To speak of the kingdom was to invoke the vision of God. God was understood to be acting in a way that would eventuate in an ultimate end of the status quo; his transcendence was received as a miracle on the way to fruition; his judging and his demand for purity led to the inclusion of some unlikely partners in festivity. Jesus' nonscriptural focus was as strong as the Essenes' anticipation of the victory of the sons of light, as the rabbis' devotion

---

11. The hyperbolic comparison of start and finish is also evident in the parable of the leaven (Matt. 13:33; Luke 13:20–21).

12. See Chilton, *Galilean Rabbi*, 101–7.

to the Torah, as Philo's discovery of pure, soul-healing philosophy. In each case, the mode of interpretation was firmly rooted within early Judaism, in the correlation between Scripture and the divine significance that the texts were held to attest.

The Resurrection as Hermeneutics

A reader arrives at the meaning (or meanings) of a text by interpreting it. The word "hermeneutics" comes from the Greek term that means "interpretation" (*hermēneia*), but it has come to refer in contemporary discussion to the general theory of meaning that a person might bring to the act of interpretation. Among the rabbis, the principle of the written and oral Torah is such a theory; for Philo, the hermeneutical key is his notion of the divine reason that underlies all thought and that comes to best expression in Scripture. The generation of the form of *Pesher* at Qumran shows that, there too, distinctive hermeneutics — involved with the group's ultimate triumph — were consciously deployed.

Jesus' interpretation, at least within the period of his lifetime, does not seem to have been a matter of an articulated theory of hermeneutics. In the course of preaching, teaching, and/or disputing, his reference to Scripture appears to have been instrumental in the limited sense that it was used to prove or illustrate a point. Usually that point concerned the kingdom of God, but he expressed no theory — at least none that is on record — of how the kingdom and Scripture were related to one another. For all his skill in the art of parable and his awareness of Targumic traditions, his intellectual achievement is simply not on the order of the Essenes', Philo's, or the rabbis'.

Indeed, the absence of an articulated theory of meaning in Jesus' use of Scripture helps to account for two characteristic features of his movement. The first is that Jesus himself was active in towns and villages in Galilee but not in cities (apart from Jerusalem) and not in formal association with a larger group such as the Essenes or the Pharisees. He was a rabbi in the sense of a local "master," a teacher who had views on purity and behavior, as well as his own favorite theme (the kingdom).

He had neither the sophisticated audience nor the intense inter-action with alternative hermeneutics that caused other teachers to spell out their own theory of interpretation. The second characteristic of his movement, the tendency to disagree in her-meneutical terms (as we have seen in the previous chapter), is also explicable if Jesus himself had no articulated hermeneu-tics. After all, had he formally claimed to transcend all law (for example), Paul would have had no dispute in Antioch.

But at this point we encounter a paradox. If, as seems certain, Jesus' principal focus — which he used Scripture to express — was the kingdom of God, how did he himself come to be the hermeneutical principle invoked by James, Paul, and Peter in their various ways? (The same question has often been put in other terms: How did the preacher of the kingdom become the principal subject of what was preached?) This paradox may only be resolved by considering the events at the end of Jesus' life.

Jesus' Last Meals and His Occupation of the Temple

The last supper was not the only supper, just the last one.[13] In fact, the last supper would have had no meaning apart from Jesus' well-established custom of eating with people socially. There was nothing unusual about a rabbi making social eat-ing an instrument of his instruction, and it was part of Jesus' method from the early days of his movement in Galilee.

Within Judaism, meals were regular expressions of social sol-idarity and of common identity as the people of God. Many sorts of meal are attested in the literature of early Judaism. From Qumran we learn of banquets at which the commu-nity convened in order of hierarchy; among the Pharisees we hear of collegial meals shared within fellowships (*haburoth*) at which like-minded fellows (*haberim*) would share the foods and the company they considered pure. Ordinary households might

---

13. For a full treatment of Jesus' teaching in regard to the worship of Israel and of what he did in the Temple, see Bruce Chilton, *The Temple of Jesus: His Sacrificial Program within a Cultural History of Sacrifice* (University Park: Penn-sylvania State University Press, 1992). The generation of eucharistic texts is analyzed in Bruce Chilton, *A Feast of Meanings: Eucharistic Theologies from Jesus through Johannine Circles*, Supplements to Novum Testamentum 72 (Leiden: Brill, 1994).

welcome the coming of the Sabbath with a prayer of sanctification (*kiddush*) over a cup of wine and open a family occasion with a blessing (*berakhah*) over bread and wine.

Jesus' meals were similar in some ways to several of these meals, but they were also distinctive. He had a characteristic understanding of what the meals meant and of who should participate in them. For him, eating socially with others in Israel was a parable of the feast in the kingdom that was to come. The idea that God would offer festivity for all peoples on his holy mountain was a key feature in the fervent expectations of Judaism during the first century, and Jesus shared that hope, as in the saying from "Q" we have considered (Matt. 8:11; Luke 13:28, 29).

Eating was a way of enacting the kingdom of God, of practicing the generous rule of the divine king. As a result, Jesus avoided exclusive practices, which in his mind divided the people of God from one another; he was willing to accept as companions people such as tax agents and other suspicious characters and to receive notorious sinners at table. The meal for him was a sign of the kingdom of God, and all the people of God, assuming they sought forgiveness, were to have access to it.

Jesus' practice of fellowship at meals caused opposition from those whose understanding of Israel was exclusive. To them, he seemed profligate, willing to eat and drink with anyone, as Jesus himself observed in a saying also from "Q":

> A man came eating and drinking, and they complain:
> Look, a glutton and drunkard,
> a fellow of tax agents and sinners.
> (see Matt. 11:19; Luke 7:34)

Many of Jesus' pharisaic opponents saw the purity of Israel as something that could only be guarded by separating from others, as in the meals of their fellowships (*ḥaburoth*). Jesus' view of purity was different. He held that a son or daughter of Israel, by virtue of being of Israel, could approach his table, or even worship in the Temple. Where necessary, repentance beforehand could be demanded, and Jesus taught his followers to pray for forgiveness daily, but his understanding was that Israelites as such were pure and were fit to offer purely of their own within the sacrificial worship of Israel.

As long as Jesus' activity was limited to Galilee, he was involved in active but essentially inconsequential disputes. Slightly deviant rabbis in Galilee were far from uncommon. But Jesus also brought his teaching into the Temple, where he insisted upon his own teaching (or *halakhah*) of purity. The incident that reflects the resulting dispute is usually called the cleansing of the Temple (Matt. 21:12–13; Mark 11:15–17; Luke 19:45–46; John 2:13–17). From the point of view of the authorities there, what Jesus was after was the opposite of cleansing. He objected to the presence of merchants who had been given permission by Caiaphas to sell sacrificial animals in the vast, outer court of the Temple. His objection was based on his own, peasant's view of purity: Israel should not offer priests' produce that they handed over money for, but should offer their own sacrifices that they brought into the Temple. He believed so vehemently what he taught that he and his followers drove the animals and the sellers out of the great court, no doubt with the use of force.

Jesus' interference in the ordinary worship of the Temple might have been sufficient by itself to bring about his execution. After all, the Temple was the center of Judaism for as long as it stood. Roman officials were so interested in its smooth functioning at the hands of the priests they appointed that they were known to sanction the penalty of death for gross sacrilege. Yet there is no indication that Jesus was arrested immediately. Instead, he remained at liberty for some time and was finally taken into custody just after one of his meals, the last supper. The decision of the authorities of the Temple to move against Jesus when they did, is what made the last supper last.

Why did the authorities wait, and why did they act when they did? The Gospels portray them as fearful of the popular backing that Jesus enjoyed, and his inclusive teaching of purity probably did bring enthusiastic followers into the Temple with him. But in addition there was another factor: Jesus could not simply be dispatched as a cultic criminal. He was not attempting an onslaught upon the Temple as such; his dispute with the authorities concerned purity within the Temple. Other rabbis of his period also engaged in physical demonstrations of the purity they required in the conduct of worship. One of them, for example, is said once to have driven thousands of sheep into the Temple, so that people could offer sacrifice in the manner he approved of (in the Babylonian Talmud, see Beza 20A, B). Jesus' action was extreme but not totally without precedent, even in the use of force.

The delay of the authorities, then, was understandable. We could also say it was commendable, reflecting continued controversy over the merits of Jesus' teaching and whether his occupation of the great court should be condemned out of hand. But why did they finally arrest Jesus? The last supper provides the key; something about Jesus' meals after his occupation of the Temple caused Judas to inform on Jesus. Of course, "Judas" is the only name that the traditions of the New Testament have left us in regard to this act of informing. We cannot say who or how many of the disciples became disaffected by Jesus' behavior after his occupation of the Temple.

However they learned of Jesus' new interpretation of his meals of fellowship, the authorities arrested him just after the supper we call last. Jesus continued to celebrate fellowship at table as a foretaste of the kingdom, just as he had before. But he also added a new and scandalous dimension of meaning. His occupation of the Temple having failed, Jesus said over the wine, "This is my blood," and over the bread, "This is my flesh" (Matt. 26:26, 28; Mark 14:22, 24; Luke 22:19–20; 1 Cor. 11:24–25; Justin, *Apology* 1.66.3).

In Jesus' context, the context of his confrontation with the authorities of the Temple, his words can have had only one meaning. He cannot have meant, "Here are my personal body and blood," because that would have been deliberately blasphemous. The Mishnah, in an effort to conceive of a heinous defect on the part of a priest involved in slaughtering the red heifer, pictures him as intending to eat the flesh or drink the blood (Parah 4:3); reference to human blood and flesh could only have made matters worse. Jesus' point was rather that, in the absence of a Temple that permitted his view of purity to be practiced, wine was his blood of sacrifice, and bread was his flesh of sacrifice. In Aramaic, "blood" (*d^ema*) and "flesh" (*bisra*, which may also be rendered as "body") can carry such a sacrificial meaning, and in Jesus' context, that is the most natural meaning.

The meaning of "the last supper," then, actually evolved over a series of meals after Jesus' occupation of the Temple. During that period, Jesus claimed that wine and bread were a better sacrifice than what was offered in the Temple: at least wine and bread were Israel's own, not tokens of priestly dominance. No wonder the opposition to him, even among the twelve (in the shape of Judas, according to the Gospels), became deadly. In essence, Jesus made his meals into a rival altar.

Jesus' Meals after His Death

The crucifixion was not an expression of general or theoretical distaste over Jesus, and still less a plot motivated by jealousy. The issues at stake were stark: God accepted either Jesus' meals of fellowship in anticipation of the kingdom or the innovations of Caiaphas in the Temple, but not both. The controversy between Jesus and the authorities in the Temple went beyond the point of compromise at the time.[14] They could agree that only one side could speak of what made sacrifice acceptable, but on little else.

The crucifixion did not resolve the controversy, but it should have ended it. The priestly authorities — who were also civil authorities by agreement with the Romans — used their political power swiftly and effectively to put down what they saw as an attack on the Temple itself. The Romans, in their turn, could only have agreed that the status quo in the Temple should be preserved. After all, Caesar himself arranged for sacrifice to be offered in the Temple on behalf of his welfare and Rome's. That arrangement — the equivalent of a loyalty oath — was crucial to the settlement with Rome. Caiaphas and Pilate acted rationally and in accordance with an established policy of mutual accommodation.

What should have ended the problem, of course, did no such

---

14. Later, of course, a James or a Peter would find such a compromise possible (and in James's case, necessary).

thing. Jesus' resurrection is variously attested in the Gospels, but a summary is given at the beginning of Acts that in fact points to the common denominator of the accounts: Jesus presented himself as alive to his apostles after he had died by various demonstrations, appearing to them, speaking of the kingdom, and sharing fellowship at meals (Acts 1:3–4a; see also the speech of Peter in Acts 10:34–43). The Gospels that give full accounts of appearances of the risen Jesus (Luke 24:13–49; John 20:1–21:23) do so on the usual understanding that gatherings that involved meals were where Jesus was known as alive.

How could one speak of a person risen from the dead? Accounts of his resurrection show in detail that Jesus was depicted, along the lines Acts 1:3–4a suggests, as showing himself alive in various ways. That variety should not be minimized; the accounts do not agree whether Jesus was instantly recognizable or even whether his resurrected body was a body of ordinary flesh. Their consensus, however, is no less stunning; Jesus is held to be personally and tangibly present in meals after his death.

Accounts of the resurrected Jesus were passed on among insiders, for people in (or near) the movement of Jesus who had accepted at least the idea that he was alive still. The audience for such stories would have included a range of people, from those who wondered whether he could be alive to those who had themselves experienced him as such, but there would be a common recognition that his rising from the dead was a meaningful concept.

There is a simple litmus test for the presence or absence of Christian faith. It does not involve abstraction or doctrine or a specific theory of hermeneutics. The test is whether one perceives that Jesus was not defeated on the cross and broke the bonds of death in order to present himself as alive to his followers. His presence in fellowship with his disciples was the vindication of what he had said concerning the kingdom of God. Jesus was right: God was indeed gathering his people. Killing the messenger only demonstrated how right he had been, because now death was shown not to be an obstacle to his continued, personal presence with his followers in celebration of the kingdom.

In the New Testament, at the end of a generation of development, the kingdom remained God's realm: ultimate, transcendent, perfect, holy, inclusive. But he who had at first preached the kingdom was now at the forefront, explicitly and without compromise, as the means — and the only means — of access to the kingdom. The stark character of that development is measurable by the phrase "kingdom of Christ," used interchangeably with "kingdom of God."[15] The latest documents of the New Testament in the present case simply identify a systemic principle that had been active since Jesus was perceived as raised from the dead.

The resurrection of Jesus is the hermeneutics of the kingdom because he must be perceived as alive for the kingdom to be felt as effective, and if the kingdom is effective, then he is alive. The identification of Jesus with the kingdom was, of course, a function of his activity in Galilee and Jerusalem. But more crucially, the very content of the resurrection was that Jesus was himself the force and reality of the kingdom, not merely its most ardent preacher.

Conclusion

The kingdom of God was both the theme of Jesus during his public activity and the content of the experience of Jesus as risen among his disciples. At first, Jesus' emphasis might be seen to be comparable to the thematic emphases of other Judaic interpreters, such as the Essenes, the Pharisees, and teachers of Wisdom. The theoretical sophistication of those groups is

---

15. The earliest such usage appears in Col. 1:13, one of the letters attributed to Paul but emanating from the circle of Timothy around 90 C.E. The putative authors — Paul and Timothy together (1:1, 2) — give thanks to the Father for making believers worthy "of a share of the portion of saints in the light, who delivered us from the authority of the darkness and transferred us into the kingdom of the son of his love" (1:12, 13). The continuity with Pauline emphases is obvious here, as is the statement from approximately five years later in Eph. 5:5, where the putative Paul speaks of those who do not have "an inheritance in the kingdom of Christ and of God." For usages during the same general period, see Rev. 11:15; 12:10 (cf. 1:9); 2 Pet. 1:11. The turn of phrase seems to have influenced the Gospel according to John, as well, when Jesus refers to "my kingdom" (18:36).

not evident in the case of Jesus, but the principle of a focus alongside Scripture, which discloses Scripture's meaning,
is comparable.

The absence of an intellectual agenda from Jesus' instrumental reference to Scripture made it possible for the major figures
in his movement who came after him — his disciple Peter,
his brother James, his interpreter Paul — to develop their own
hermeneutics. But as they did so, they manifested a common
awareness, not simply of Jesus as risen from the dead, but of
Jesus as risen in order to warrant the triumphal news of the
kingdom.

Part of what makes Christianity seem opaque to outsiders is
that the intellection that is characteristic of rabbinic Judaism is
absent from Jesus' teaching. He is articulate but not theoretical.
He is not presented as the conscious agent of a system, in the
manner of Moses or Mohammed. He asserts that God is acting
in and through human beings and that God's activity is final,
transcendent, demanding, pure, and inclusive. God is gathering.

How does he gather, and whom? Where are they being
brought to?

He answers such questions in metaphors and parables. He
demands intellection without providing a system of his own.
The diversity of Christian faith, then and now, is an inevitable
outcome of Jesus' teaching. Yet within that diversity, the common perception of Jesus' triumph over the grave as the seal of
the kingdom is the guarantee of integrity. God cares only for
the response to the kingdom, by means of acknowledging the
kingdom's agent. Everything else is ancillary: not only wealth
and status and power and learning, but even virtue of the most
modest sort. Everything but the kingdom is under suspicion because anything — even self-righteous virtue — might be used to
draw us from the kingdom of God and of his Christ.

6

The Interpretative Resolution of the New Testament

Jesus interpreted Scripture by means of the kingdom, and his followers interpreted the kingdom by means of the resurrection. Once those fundamentals have been understood, the differences and contradictions among James, Paul, and Peter — as well as their underlying consensus — become explicable. Their common reference is to the kingdom and to Jesus as its agent, and their common assumption is that both are to be found in Scripture; this is the sine qua non of Christianity. But how are that kingdom and this Jesus to be related to Israel, to the covenant with the patriarchs, to the promises to David, and to Scripture itself? Only on the basis of a properly hermeneutical theory, the very thing Jesus did not leave his followers, could such questions be answered.

James, Paul, and Peter represent the beginning of Christian intellectual traditions, and, as we have seen, their differences go far beyond whether the preferred comparison with Jesus is David, Abraham, or Moses. Each comparison is worked out in the service of a distinct social policy, within a characteristic understanding of the significance of Scripture, and toward a Christology that is all its own. The existence of churches in contact with one another, founded by representatives of the three major teachers of the time, or one of the three personally, assured that the issue of consensus would arise. Was early Christianity a single movement, a Church, or a series of isolated, largely incompatible communities? If Jesus and the resurrection represented a seismic shift in the constitution of Judaism, was the result a new foundation or a heap of rubble?

Paul put that question masterfully to the Corinthians around 55 C.E.:

> I appeal to you, brothers, by the name of our Lord Jesus Christ, so that you all agree and that there be no schisms among you, but that you be restored in the same mind and the same judgment. For it has been made clear to me, my brothers, by those around Chloe, that there are contentions among you. I mean this, that each of you says, "I am Paul's," or "I am Apollos's," or "I am Cephas's," or "I am Christ's." Is Christ divided? Was Paul crucified for you? Were you baptized into the name of Paul? (1 Cor. 1:10–13)

No less than in the case of his letter to the Galatians, Paul's mastery of rhetoric should not be confused with his control over the situation.

The passage shows that there was in fact a fission in the community: that is, there were groups known according to the teachers to whom they showed loyalty, Paul himself, Apollos,[1] and Cephas. Apparently, one group even claimed that it alone was familiar with the way of Christ.[2] Paul's appeal to unity is made in the context of diversity and antagonism. If we consider the fissions reflected in Galatians together with what Paul says here, there is only one answer to the question "Is Christ divided?" and Paul would not much have liked to hear it.

By focusing on Jesus' crucifixion and believers' baptism, Paul points to the factor that has perennially compelled Christians to seek unity in the midst of obvious diversity, often in the face of ridicule and opposition. A single Lord was crucified, and learning that narrative (in the form of a gospel, prior to

---

1. Apollos is said in the book of Acts to have known "only the baptism of John [the Baptist]" (Acts 18:24–19:7) before he accepted correction. The passage in Corinthians would suggest that his influence and his differences from Paul have been glossed over in Acts.

2. The similarity with rivalries among Christian groups during the history of the Church is obvious.

one's baptism), Christians are baptized into the reality of a single, risen Lord and his kingdom. The unity of the Church has never been a sociological fact in any era (nostalgic histories to the contrary). But in every time and place in which reflection on Christian faith and practice has been possible, theology has been ecumenical because the attempt has been made to address the whole inhabited world (the *oikoumene*) with the claims of "One Lord, one faith, one baptism, one God and father of all, above all and through all and in all" (Eph. 4:5–6).[3]

In order to make those claims plausible, it was necessary at least to attempt to develop a common preparation for baptism, a standard for the practice of initiation. That standard is represented in the New Testament by what are known as the Synoptic Gospels (Matthew, Mark, and Luke). The first three Gospels emerged from the catechetical stage of the movement, when candidates were prepared for baptism; they provide the best indications of the governing concerns of the Church as it initiated new members.

The Synoptic Gospels

The first three Gospels are called "synoptic" in scholarly discussion because they may be viewed together when they are printed in columns. Unfortunately, this obvious literary relationship has caused scholars to presume that they were composed by scribes working in isolation who copied, one from another. A comparative approach,[4] served by an understanding of the development of tradition into documents within both early Judaism and Christianity, has brought us to the point where deviations of one document from another related document are not assumed to be purely scribal changes. After all, the Gospels were not written by individual scholars for a learned public. Rather, agreements and disagreements among the Syn-

---

3. Ephesians was written after Paul's time (ca. 95 C.E.) but in his name, and it is a lucid development of his theology.

4. For what follows, see Bruce Chilton, *Profiles of a Rabbi: Synoptic Opportunities in Reading about Jesus*, Brown Judaic Studies 177 (Atlanta: Scholars Press, 1989).

optic Gospels provide a way to see how different communities of Christians pursued a common program of catechism, but in distinctive ways.

Material agreement among the Gospels is no surprise because documents of early Judaism and rabbinic Judaism also present synoptic relationships, sometimes with greater verbal similarity and often with more than three documents involved. What is notable in the synoptic character of the first three Gospels is that the orders of passages, one after another, can be compared regularly; this justifies their literary characterization as the "Synoptics." But once their function within catechesis is appreciated, the cause of their agreements and of their deviation from one another becomes evident. What we see in the first three Gospels are the methods of baptismal initiation followed in three influential, nearly contemporaneous, but separate churches. Contact among the communities may be assumed to have been by both oral and written means, given the evidence regarding communication within early Christian communities. In time, some of the most important communities produced their catechisms as written standards, the Synoptic Gospels as we know them today. There is a reasonable degree of consensus that Mark was the first of the Gospels to be written, around 71 C.E. in the environs of Rome. As convention has it, Matthew was subsequently composed, near 80 C.E., perhaps in Damascus (or elsewhere in Syria), while Luke came later, say, in 90 C.E., perhaps in Antioch.

The Synoptic Gospels are written simply; only Luke aspires to (and even then does not reach) a good, literary standard of Greek. Their genius, in aggregate, lies not in their quality as published products. After all, their intended sphere of usage was limited; they were addressed to communities of Christians, not to the world of literature. Their genius, rather, lies in their development as an ecumenical tool, where they focus on the nexus between the kingdom and Jesus as the center of common catechesis throughout the Church. They fixed upon the common ground of the hermeneutics of resurrection by transforming the meaning of the kingdom. The transformation is sufficiently general so that the peculiarities of each Synoptic Gospel may be described as a variation on a theme, while it is so distinctive that no other ancient document (Christian or not) may be described as sharing it.

The Synoptic transformation of the meaning of the kingdom introduces the kingdom as preached by Jesus (Matt. 4:17, 23; 9:35; 12:28; Mark 1:15; Luke 4:43; 8:1; 9:2; 10:9, 11; 11:20). This obvious feature of the Gospels' narratives is no less influential for being evident: the kingdom from this point onward is established as the burden of Jesus' message and Jesus' message only. Accepting him means accepting the kingdom, and vice versa.

The next major phase in the Synoptic transformation of the kingdom is explanatory. The Jesus who is the kingdom's herald is also its advocate, who explains its features to those who hear and yet are puzzled (or even scandalized). The extent of the material each Gospel devotes to this phase varies greatly, but in every case it is the largest phase.[5] The distribution of this material also varies, but it is striking that none of the Synoptic Gospels invokes the term "kingdom" as a link to include all statements on the subject in a single complex of material. Such an association by catchword is indeed detectable over short runs of material, so that isolated sayings are the exception, not the rule, but in no case is subject matter or wording used to present all the sayings about the kingdom in a single unit. Rather, narrative contexts are developed in which Jesus' activity in preaching, teaching, and disputing becomes the governing framework for a given run of sayings.

Those frameworks vary from Gospel to Gospel, of course, as do the individual sayings presented; the distribution of sayings can certainly not be explained by reference to some fixed, historical, or scribal ordering. The point is rather that the typically Synoptic transformation of Jesus' preaching embeds the kingdom within his ministry, so that he and the kingdom become approximately interchangeable. The particular textual moves that achieve this identification vary; the fact that it is achieved does not.

---

5. Matthew 5:3, 10, 19, 20; 6:10, 33; 7:21; 8:11, 12; 11:12; 13:11, 19, 24, 31, 33, 38, 41, 43, 44, 45, 47, 52; 16:19; 18:1, 3, 4, 23; 19:12, 14, 23; 20:1; 21:31, 43; 22:2; 23:14; 24:14; 25:1, 34; Mark 4:11, 26, 30; 9:1, 47; 10:14, 15, 23, 24, 25; 12:34; Luke 6:20; 7:28; 8:1, 10; 9:11, 27, 60, 62; 11:2; 12:31; 13:18, 20, 28, 29; 16:16; 17:20, 21; 18:16, 17, 24, 25, 29; 21:31.

The last phase of the Synoptic transformation of the kingdom pursues the logic of the identification; Jesus' death and the kingdom are presented as mutually explicating. "I shall not drink of the fruit of the vine again, until I drink it with you new in God's kingdom" (cf. Matt. 26:29; Mark 14:25; Luke 22:18). Within the Synoptics that saying serves to insist that the same Jesus who announced and taught the kingdom is also the sole guarantor of its glorious coming. His presence in eucharistic meals, eating and drinking with his disciples anew, is the seal of the kingdom's fruition.

The Synoptic transformation of the kingdom can be found in a unique pattern of the distribution of sayings and of their narrative contexts within Jesus' ministry. The result is to focus in an innovative fashion upon Jesus as the herald, the advocate, and the guarantor of the kingdom. Arguably, the transformation explicates what is implicit within the sayings tradition ("Q"): an awareness that Jesus' ministry is a seal of the kingdom.

The most obvious instance of such a claim within his sayings is Jesus' observation concerning his exorcisms and the kingdom (Matt. 12:28; Luke 11:20). But the emphasis even here falls more on the kingdom than on Jesus, so that the saying only heightens by contrast the Synoptic transformation, in which Jesus' preaching of the kingdom becomes the seal of his divine mission, not the principal point at issue. He who witnessed the kingdom is, within the Synoptics, attested as God's son by virtue of his unique message. Precisely because a signal adjustment of precedence between Jesus and the kingdom has taken place, the language of "transformation" is appropriate.

When this sense of the kingdom is compared with that in other documents of early Judaism and Christianity, the Synoptic transformation can be seen as a particular framing of Jesus' sayings and narratives, not merely a loose characterization of similar material in three Gospels. How the transformation was effected, whether by literary borrowing from one document to another or by the sharing of now lost antecedents, is a matter of conjecture.[6] What is plain, however, is that the Synoptics

---

6. The history of such speculation is impressively given objective standing

embody the first ecumenical catechesis, and their place in the canon is the seal of their success.

The Synoptic Hermeneutics of Scripture

How does Scripture relate us to the living Christ, whose rising from the dead substantiates the reality of the kingdom? For some fifteen years, a revival of interest in the historical Jesus has shown itself in published books and articles. But they usually do not address the question of faith: What is there about the Gospels, in their stories about one rabbi from Galilee, that lays claim to our experience of God now? When we think historically about religion, we refer to evidence in order to draw inferences; our guiding purpose is to describe what has happened, what has been taught, what has been believed, in the past. But our faith is not thirsty for a description of that kind. Our belief, or our quest for belief, is a matter of what we see God doing to and with our lives in the present. The Synoptic transformation addressed just that concern.

The Synoptics even cast present faith in a role of importance because it is leading to a climactic future. The seed of faith sprouting on the ground now can only be appreciated in the light of the harvest that is to come (Matt. 13:1–9; Mark 4:1–9; Luke 8:4–8). The past may be of intellectual interest, but it is off center from the perspective of faith. The focus of Jesus as presented by the Synoptic Gospels is the kingdom of God: the power of God on behalf of his people that transforms their lives now and that is one day to be all in all.

Because the religious truth of the Gospels is not the same thing as historical information about Jesus, belief requires a reading of Scripture that is not just a matter of historical description. Many recent studies of Jesus are deficient precisely because they do not deal with the topic of the previous chapter: what Jesus himself did with the Bible of his time, the Scriptures of Israel.

---

by referring to it as "the Synoptic problem," as if it were a phenomenon of texts rather than a disturbance among interpreters.

How can scholars ignore Jesus' treatment of Scripture when his teaching is filled with biblical references and allusions? The basic answer seems to be that Jesus the preacher simply does not fit the role that scholarly fashion would like to assign to him.

Some scholars emphasize the extent to which Galilee was a pluralistic environment, but they forget that specifically Jewish towns and villages, such as those frequented by Jesus, were a part of that pluralism. Their Jesus is a Hellenistic philosopher, who can have little to do with the Scriptures and traditions of Israel. Other scholars correctly emphasize the Judaic environment of Jesus, but they then attempt to argue that Jesus was so concerned with a ministry of healing that Scripture was not his focus. Their Jesus is theoretically Jewish, but he is unlike the many rabbis of his period who were renowned both for teaching and for deeds of power.

If an especial concern of the Synoptics is with how Christ is brought to expression by means of the Scriptures, it is obvious that attempts to portray Jesus as anything but a preacher are unable to provide a plausible interpretation of them (or of him). In fact (as we have seen in the last chapter), Jesus' approach to Scripture made him distinctive among rabbis of his time and also set in motion a movement of biblical interpretation that produced the New Testament. The Synoptics, having identified the common ground of a hermeneutics of resurrection as the dynamic of Christian interpretation, proceed to exemplify how to apply it.

The story of the confession of Peter at Caesarea Philippi (Matt. 16:13–23; Mark 8:27–33; Luke 9:18–22) presents an example of Synoptic instruction in reading with faith. Jesus himself poses the question of his identity in the opening ("Who do people say I am?" in Mark), and the disciples reply with a startling range of biblically based answers. He is said to be John the baptizer, Elijah, or one of the prophets. In seeing Jesus in the Bible, and the Bible in Jesus, the disciples immediately introduce us to a use of Scripture that is out of the ordinary. The prophets are not referred to as purely historical but are taken to be alive and effective in the ministry of Jesus.

The common element in these understandings is that they involve an approach to the Bible as a matter of experience. Jesus is seen in directly prophetic terms; the prophets' activity lives on in the case of Jesus. Jesus was a catalyst for his followers and in the memory of the Church; he set off a reaction between the Bible of the time and those who read the Bible. When people experienced Jesus, biblical language and imagery became the vehicle of understanding and expressing what was happening. Similarly, Jesus had taken his principal theme, the kingdom of God, from the Bible of his day (the Aramaic paraphrases known as the Targums). For him (as we have seen) the kingdom was not simply a promise contained in the Bible but a reality that was changing the world. The principle that the Scripture refers to facts of experience was accepted by those who tried to understand Jesus as one of the prophets.

But Jesus in the Synoptic narrative is not content with a simple identification of himself with one of the prophets of old; he replies, "But who do you yourselves say I am?" The question is also a demand. The demand of Jesus is to use the measure of Scripture in a critical way, not only as a matter of experience. His disciples are to see him as an important figure like John, Elijah, or another prophet, but also as crucially different.

By refusing to embrace any one prophetic designation in the story, Jesus presses Peter on to use the title "Christ," one of the most flexible terms in the Hebrew Bible. Its associations of empowered anointing are evident, but Jesus then proceeds to relate the term to his own suffering. A criticism of the received understanding of Scripture is obvious here: it simply will not do to identify Jesus merely with the charisma of the prophets or with the might of a messiah. Jesus in the story insists on his difference from such figures.

His difference, his individuality, does not reside in his claim to be greater than an Elijah or any anticipated messiah. After all, Jesus did not expect to be taken up alive into heaven, as was said of Elijah (see 2 Kings 2:9–12), and no one ever said that he actually ruled as the Messiah of Israel. Jesus' distinctiveness is a matter of his suffering, which the story of Caesarea Philippi places alongside the prophetic and messianic designations as the key to Jesus' identity. The Synoptic Jesus insists not only that Scripture be seen as a matter of experience but that the critical difference between present experience and the biblical testimony is as important for our understanding of God as the similarity between the two.

In a single word, there is an *analogy* between Jesus and the figures of the Hebrew Bible. He is experienced in terms of what they were, and yet he is also seen as different; and in that difference lies the meaning of his teaching and his action. Jesus liked to refer to Scripture as fulfilled in his ministry.[7] He called attention to both similarities and critical distinctions between what was said of God in Scripture and what he saw of God as a matter of experience. The promises to Israel might lead one to expect that the feast of the kingdom was to exclude those outside the nation, but Jesus anticipated that people would stream in from everywhere and that exclusions would be surprising (see Matt. 8:11, 12; Luke 13:28, 29, as discussed in the last chapter). The analogy between Scripture and experience is rooted in the sensibility that a given biblical text is identifying and describing the God we experience. But under Jesus' approach there is no sense in which Scripture can be said to limit what God does and is about to do.

The experience of God as biblical is only the beginning, or the occasion, of the Bible's authority. Jesus refused to limit himself to the repetition of the biblical text: he was noted (and notorious) for departing from agreed norms in order to speak of God. Who else within his time and setting would compare the kingdom of the One, Almighty God with a woman baking bread (Luke 13:20–21)? In addition to being experiential in reference to Scripture, Jesus was also critical. His critical perspective, of course, was not historical; rather, his creative adaptation of biblical language and imagery evidences an awareness that God in the text and God in experience do not entirely coincide.

Because the God of the Bible is experienced and yet — as experienced — may not be contained by the biblical text, the trademark of Jesus' instrumental use of Scripture is "fulfillment." By referring to Scripture as fulfilled, Jesus claimed to resolve the tension between the coincidence and the distance of the biblical God in relation to his own experience. When, for

---

7. See Matt. 3:15; 5:17; 23:32: 26:54, 56; Mark 14:49; Luke 4:21; 24:44.

example, Jesus says in the synagogue in Nazareth, "Today this Scripture has been fulfilled in your ears," he does not literally mean that he did everything referred to in the passage from Isaiah he has just read (see Luke 4:16–21). The simple facts are that Isaiah 61:1, 2 refers to things Jesus never did, such as releasing prisoners from jail, and that Jesus did things the text makes no mention of, such as declaring people free of impurity (see Matt. 8:2–4; Mark 1:40–45; Luke 5:12–16).

By means of their example, the Synoptic Gospels establish a thoroughly christological technique in the interpretation of Scripture. Christ, the guarantor of the kingdom, is the standard by which Scripture is experienced, corrected, and understood to have been fulfilled. There is here still no articulated theory of the relationship between Christ and Scripture; that would come later. But the Synoptics did insist that the catechesis of believers who sought baptism should include the christological technique of understanding the Scriptures.

Much as in the case of Peter's interpretation, the Synoptic approach is curiously indeterminate at the level of social policy. In order to predict whether a given element of the Hebrew Bible would be commended or set aside, one would need to know what image of Christ was being used as the standard of judgment. The text is related to the finished product of interpretation as a quarry is related to an engagement ring. There is no bias apparent toward the position of a James or a Paul. Indeed, there is even less predisposition toward any normative status of the Hebrew Bible than in Petrine interpretation, because Moses is not accorded a central position.

The Synoptics' hermeneutics are not a compromise: they are the outcome of an evolution of technique. Nonetheless, they are open to the application of widely variant social policies, and that appears to have been part of the secret of their success. Because Antioch was the crucible where the great figures of primitive Christianity brought their differences to the most critical point, Antioch is best seen as the center where the Synoptic catechesis was first developed. It was then swiftly accepted (and adapted) in other major centers of what now indeed was a Church with a certain standard of catechesis.

Among those who might have been responsible for the Synoptic breakthrough, the most likely teacher is Barnabas. Unlike Paul, he remained in the vicinity of Antioch long after the famous confrontation, and his continued activity involved a dispute with Paul (see Acts 15:36–41). His position is most similar to Peter's, and yet the advance of interpretation at the level of technique suggests a new mind at work. Finally, there is attributed to Barnabas an epistle (from the second century) that is centrally concerned with the relationship between Christ, the Scriptures, and institutions of Judaism.[8] That would seem to be a continuation of his original contribution, the Synoptic hermeneutics of Scripture.

Matthew, Mark, Luke, and John

Once the Synoptic catechesis was accepted within communities, it was subjected to local developments. The result is the close relationship of and the striking differences between Matthew, Mark, and Luke. Each of the Gospels, in turn, represents a distinctive application of the same basic technique of scriptural interpretation that was established in the Synoptic catechesis by Barnabas.

Mark, the first of the Gospels to be written, was produced within the context of mounting persecution in Rome and of increasing separation from synagogues. Its reference to Scripture is largely uninventive, determined by the tradition handed on to Rome. In the midst of immediate and pressing social concerns — the suspicion of civil authorities and the growing antagonism of Judaic leaders — the relationship between Christ and Scripture was not a focal topic. Nonetheless, the Gospel does manifest, in its opening chapter, a desire to simplify the issue.

Introducing the ministry of John the Baptist, Mark 1:2–3 reads:

---

8. See Leslie W. Barnard, *Studies in the Apostolic Fathers and Their Background* (Oxford: Blackwell, 1966); Robert A. Kraft, *Barnabas and the Didache* (New York: Nelson, 1965).

> Just as it is written in Isaiah, the prophet —
> Behold, I send my messenger before your face,
> who will prepare your way.
> A voice of one crying in the wilderness,
> prepare the way of the Lord, make straight his paths.

The language of the "voice of one crying in the wilderness" is in fact Isaian,[9] but the reference to the "messenger" is from a different book altogether: Malachi (3:1).

Within the usage of Jesus and Barnabas, there was no reason to call attention to one biblical book, because two were being drawn upon. Mark here represents a desire to tie the relation between Christ and Scripture more tightly, to relate one passage to one event involving Jesus at a time. The result, of course, is both clumsy and inaccurate, an indication that scriptural interpretation is not a vital issue here.

The Markan tendency to tighten the relationship between Christ and Scripture is pursued to a greater extent in Matthew. Matthew cites Scripture more explicitly, and more insistently says it is fulfilled by Jesus, than does any other Gospel. The citation of passages verbatim is especially striking and is somewhat reminiscent of the Essene technique of the *Pesher.*[10] But the Matthean application of Scripture to Christ is pictorial to the point that sometimes it is literalistic.

Perhaps the most famous distortion that results is the picture of Jesus riding into Jerusalem on both a donkey and its colt (Matt. 21:1–7). In the book of Zechariah (9:9), the messianic king is predicted to arrive "on an ass, on a colt the foal of an ass." Matthew is the only Synoptic Gospel that quotes the passage at length, in a Greek form, "on an ass *and* the foal of an ass." In the interests of consistency, the Matthean Jesus is then described as sitting upon both of the animals.

Luke appears to represent some actual advance in the christological technique of interpretation inherited from Barnabas.[11]

---

9. The citation is from a portion of the book (40:3) that influenced Jesus himself deeply. The Targum includes a reference to the kingdom within the same section (40:9).

10. It is likely that there were contacts between Matthew's community in Damascus and Essenes who lived there.

11. In that Luke was composed in Antioch after the time of Barnabas

There is less concern for the sort of specificity attempted in Mark and Matthew, and more for the way in which Scripture finds its fulfillment in Jesus. Luke alone of the Gospels has Jesus say to his followers prior to his arrest: "For I say to you that this writing must be fulfilled in me, 'He was reckoned among transgressors,' for that which concerns me has found its purpose" (22:37; cf. Isa. 53:12). Luke's Jesus remains free in his selection of texts, without citation, but the idea that such a Scripture's purpose or end (*telos*) is to be found in Jesus is skillfully developed.

The passage involved in Luke 22:37 is from the description of the "suffering servant" in Isaiah (53:12). That passage is important within the presentation of Luke and its companion work, the book of Acts. In Acts, Philip will convert and baptize the African official on the basis of the christological reading of Isaiah 53 (see Acts 8:26–38). The purposive relationship between Scripture and Christ is clearly marked out as a principle in effective preaching. Within Luke and Acts, that principle is the guiding program of scriptural interpretation.

John's Gospel, written in Ephesus around 100 C.E., presupposes that its readers have been baptized, following a catechesis such as the Synoptics represent. It is a far more reflective work than the first three Gospels, and it develops in its prologue (John 1:1–18) as full a statement of the relationship between Jesus and Scripture as the Gospels ever offer. It explores a distinctive vocabulary in order to articulate Jesus' impact upon humanity, a vocabulary that is largely derived from the theological language of the Targumim.

Jesus is explained in terms of God's "word," *logos* in Greek, *memra* in Aramaic. *Memra*, a nominal form of the verb "to speak" (*'amar*), is the way the Targumim refer to God's activity of commanding. God might simply be thought of as commanding what is ordered when the term is used, but the emphasis might fall on the intention behind the divine order. Then again, the usage might call attention to how and why people respond to the order. *Memra* might therefore refer to the primordial

and under relatively stable conditions, the conditions for development were favorable.

"word" of God in creating the heavens and the earth, to the revelation of the Torah, or to the disobedient response God's commands sometimes encounter. It is no coincidence that John's Gospel explains the relationship between Jesus and Scripture by means of a term whose exact significance was determined by the context in which it was used.

John's prologue presents a nuanced teaching of how Jesus Christ might be understood as a part of God's commanding *logos* or *memra*.[12] The first usage of *logos* in the Gospel simply establishes its identity with God: "In the beginning was the word, and the word was related to God, and the word was God" (1:1).[13] The word is identified as the creative, primordial source of what exists (1:2, 3), in a way quite consistent with the association of *memra* and the creation within the Targumim.

God's *logos* is next said to be the place where "life" is, and that life is held to be the "light" of all humanity (v. 4). "Light" (rather than "word") is the first directly christological category in the prologue. It is the "light" that shines in the darkness (v. 5), that enlightens every person (v. 9). John's grammar reflects *a theology of light* precisely: the "light," a neuter noun in Greek (*to phos*), is identified as masculine and singular in v. 10: "In it was the world, and the world came into existence through it, and the world did not know *him*." From that moment, the usage of pronouns and the summary reference to Jesus' ministry (vv. 11–13, cf. vv. 6–8) make it clear we are dealing with a person, not an entity. He is said to have shone at the dawn of creation within God's *logos* and yet not to have been recognized when he came to his own.

The *logos*, then, is the source of light, which is to say that in Jesus shines the *memra*, God's mighty command, vindicating and warning his people. Verse 14 refers to the *logos* as becoming flesh and then explains that assertion by saying it "dwelt among us" (*eskēnōsen en hēmin*). The verb *skēnoō*, it is often observed, relates naturally to *shakhan* in Hebrew and Aramaic, from which

---

12. For a technical discussion of the prologue in its relationship to the Targumim, see Bruce Chilton, "Typologies of *Memra* and the Fourth Gospel," *Targum Studies* 1 (1992) 89–100.

13. The preposition *pros* in Greek unequivocally means "to." The verse has less accurately been rendered in the past, "and the word was with God."

Shekhinah, the principal term of reference to God's presence in the Temple, is derived. Jesus is here held to embody God, to incarnate what before had been known only in words.

The implicit comparison between revelation in word and personal revelation is spelled out in a key section of the prologue: "For the law was given through Moses; grace and truth came through Jesus Christ" (v. 17). The connection of *logos*, taken as *memra*, to the revelation through Moses is evident. At no point and in no way does the prologue present the revelation through Jesus as disjunctive with the revelation through Moses; the underlying contention is that Jesus is the person in whom God's *logos*, his activity in creating and revealing, is manifest.

The last verse of the prologue makes Jesus' status as the personal manifestation of God explicit: "No one has at any time seen God; an only begotten, God, who was in the bosom of the father, that one has made him known" (v. 18). No one has at any time seen God, provided the reader has followed the logic of his revelation as the prologue outlines it. Jesus, as an only begotten, has made God known (*exēgēsato*). Jesus is presented as the exegesis of God, the one who speaks his word. In that role, the Fourth Gospel can refer to Jesus as God (*theos*) just as Philo so refers to Moses:[14] in order to insist that the instrument of God's word is himself to be taken as divinely valued.

John's presentation of the relationship between Jesus and God's word is demanding, as is to be expected from an advanced work such as the Fourth Gospel. But when we reduce the poetics of Johannine interpretation to the underlying theory, we find a simple formulation: Jesus makes the divine *logos* known that is also attested in Scripture, and he makes it known more truly than does Scripture, because he personally embodies God. The poetics of John are complex and moving; the hermeneutics of John are fundamentally the sequel of what we find in the Synoptics.

---

14. See *Legum Allegoria* 1.40; *De Sacrificiis Abelis et Caini* 9; *Quod Deterius Potiori insidiari soleat* 161, 162; *De Migratione Abrahami* 84; *De Mutatione Nominum* 19; *De Vita Moses* 1.158; *Quod Omnis Probus Liber sit* 43.

Hebrews and Typology

Near the time of John's Gospel, but in Alexandria rather than Ephesus, the Epistle to the Hebrews was written. It engages in a series of scriptural identifications of Jesus, none more vivid than the portrayal of Jesus as a high priest. In its elaboration of a self-consciously christological interpretation, Hebrews turns the Synoptic approach to the relationship between Jesus and Scripture into an overt theory. The devotion to detail involved attests the concern to develop that relationship fully.

Chapter 9 of Hebrews imagines the "first" scheme of sacrifice, by which is meant the Temple in Jerusalem. Specific mention is made of the menorah, the table and presented bread in the holy place, with the holy of holies empty, but for the gold censer and the ark.[15] The reference to the censer as being in the holy of holies fixes the point in time of which the author speaks: it can only be the day of atonement, when the high priest made his single visit to that sanctum, censer in hand.

This precise moment is specified only in order to be fixed, frozen forever. For Hebrews, what was a fleeting movement in the case of the high priest was an eternal truth in the case of Jesus. The movement of ordinary priests, in and out of the holy place, the "first tabernacle" (v. 6), while the high priest could only enter "the second tabernacle," the holy of holies (v. 7), once a year, was designed by the spirit of God as a parable: the way into the holy of holies could not be revealed while the first Temple, the first tabernacle and its service, continued (vv. 8–10). That way could only be opened, after the Temple was destroyed, by Christ, who became high priest and passed through "the greater and more perfect tabernacle" of his body (v. 11) by the power of his own blood (v. 12), so that he could find eternal redemption in the sanctuary.

Signal motifs within the Gospels are developed in the passage. The identification of Jesus' death and the destruction of the Temple, which the Gospels achieve in narrative terms, is

---

15. For a consideration of the terminological problems, see Harold W. Attridge, *The Epistle to the Hebrews*, Hermeneia (Philadelphia: Fortress, 1989), 230; and Brooke Foss Westcott, *The Epistle to the Hebrews* (London: Macmillan, 1909), 244–52.

assumed to be complete.[16] Moreover, the passage takes it for granted that Jesus' body was a kind of "tabernacle," an instrument of sacrifice (v. 11), apparently because the Gospels speak of his offering his body and his blood in the words of institution. (And John, of course, actually has Jesus refer to "the temple of his body" [2:21].)[17] "Body" and "blood" here are Jesus' self-immolating means to his end as high priest. In Hebrews the Temple in Jerusalem has been replaced by a purely ideological construct. The true high priest has entered once for all (v. 12) within the innermost recess of sanctity, so that no further sacrificial action is necessary or appropriate.

In Hebrews the homiletic conviction of Luke, that Scripture finds its purpose in Jesus, is elevated to the status of a theory. The hermeneutics of resurrection have now overtly become the hermeneutics of preexistence. Jesus lives because he was always alive, and in the light of his activity one can finally understand what Scripture was speaking of. The destruction of the Temple in 70 C.E. was an advantage because it enables us to distinguish the image from the reflection.

In the conception of Hebrews, the Temple on earth was a copy and shadow of the heavenly sanctuary, of which Moses had seen "types."[18] A type (*tupos* in Greek) is an impress, a derived version of a reality (the antitype). Moses had seen the very throne of God, which was then approximated on earth. That approximation is called the "first covenant" (9:15), but the heavenly sanctuary, into which Christ has entered (9:24), offers us a "new covenant" (9:15) — the truth that has been palely reflected all along.

The logic of typology, developed to a theoretical level in Hebrews, was to serve Christianity in a variety of forms until the Enlightenment. Only at that stage did criticism of the Bible appear to be corrosive of Christian faith, because the meaning of Scripture (that is, the Hebrew Bible) did not comport with

---

16. It is not even clear what exactly the author made of the interim between the two events.

17. See Westcott, *Epistle to the Hebrews*, 258–60.

18. See Heb. 8:1–6. In Hebrews, the usage of the language of typology is quite complex, although the underlying conception is fairly simple. Paul reflects an earlier form of typological interpretation in 1 Corinthians 10.

what was attributed to it from Hebrews onward. But the corrosion has been severe, to the extent that Christians today seem caught between the alternatives of denying the critical meaning of Scripture and denying Christology. For that reason, it is crucial to understand that typology, and the powerful intellectual tradition it fed, are expressions of the hermeneutics of resurrection. One way to account for the vivid awareness of the shepherd who guides us to the kingdom (see Heb. 13:20–21) is to see that he has always been there, even for those who were not aware of him.

Conclusion

According to Jesus, the principle that informed Scripture was the kingdom of God. The function of the text, particularly in its oral, Aramaic form, was to awaken hearers to the reality that God was gathering his own people, wherever they were, into the new, festive purity of eschatological fellowship with the patriarchs. Jesus' recourse to Scripture was entirely instrumental; once his hearers were aware of the kingdom, they might perceive and enjoy it in the innumerable ways his parables suggest are possible. Those parables are redolent of biblical images, but they usually do not require a knowledge of specific texts to be appreciated. Jesus' meals — themselves parabolic anticipations of the kingdom — required no precise, scriptural warrant in order to be celebrated.

Jesus' crucifixion resulted from his insistence that the eschatological purity of the kingdom superseded the arrangements of the authorities in the Temple. Their purpose, in association with the Roman governor, was to preserve the agreed status of sacrificial worship. Jesus objected to commercialism in the Temple because he believed that Israel, once forgiveness had purified them, should offer something of their own in sacrifice, rather than commodities procured by priests. His execution came about after his occupation of the Temple, when he went so far as to claim that God found his meals of fellowship preferable to sacrifice in the Temple.

Together with the kingdom, the resurrection is an indispensable postulate of Christian interpretation. When Jesus' followers experienced him as alive again during the course of their meals after the crucifixion, they understood that the kingdom's purity as he taught it had been vindicated by God. Because he was alive, the kingdom was available; because the kingdom could be discerned, he was alive.

The greatest figures in the primitive Church — Peter, James, and Paul — emerged as dominant as a result of their successful programs for initiating new members. Each developed a catechesis in which the relationship between Jesus and Scripture was distinctively worked out. The catechetical strategy of each group was cognate with its social constituency. The Petrine approach was to portray Jesus in Mosaic terms, so that the covenant of Moses and the divine sonship of Jesus stood side by side, each interpreting the other. James's perspective was more straightforward: Jesus was the scion of David, who fulfilled the promises of Torah to Israel in their commonly understood meaning. Paul challenged any common understanding of the Torah with his insistence that Abraham embodied a principle of believing that was best fulfilled by means of faith in and through Jesus Christ alone; no normative role could be attributed to the text itself.

The Synoptic tradition was framed as an ecumenical catechesis, probably by Barnabas in Antioch, in order to mediate the conflicts among communities that were influenced by teachers such as Peter, James, and Paul. The Synoptic Gospels established a thoroughly christological technique in the interpretation of Scripture. Christ, the herald, advocate, and guarantor of the kingdom, is the standard by which Scripture is experienced, corrected, and understood to have been fulfilled. There is here still no articulated theory of the relationship between Christ and Scripture; that would come later. But the Synoptics did insist that the catechesis of believers who sought baptism should include the christological technique of positing an analogy between Jesus and the Scriptures. Individual communities might work that analogy out in a Petrine, a Jacobean, or a Pauline direction, but the genius of the Synoptic catechesis is the identification of a common technique of interpretation among the great figures of the Church.

Among the Synoptic Gospels, Mark and especially Matthew manifest an attempt to simplify the relationship between Jesus and the Scriptures by positing a one-to-one correspondence between texts and events concerning Jesus. Luke more successfully elaborates a homiletic technique, identifying Jesus with the purpose behind the Scripture. It is only with John's Gospel that a theory of the relationship between Jesus and the Scriptures begins to be articulated. Borrowing a term from the Targumim (*memra*), John finds that the "word" that had been spoken in the case of Moses had been embodied in the case of Jesus. The son made plain the purpose, intent, and meaning of the wording of the law.

Scriptural interpretation in the New Testament occupies a strictly corollary position within the greater task of interpreting Jesus as the kingdom's only true agent, risen from the dead. Once that focus is appreciated within the social diversity of the early Church, the apparent variety of early Christian sources is resolved. Hebrews, composed near the end of the period, develops the sort of typology that became the dominant theory: such divine realities as the Hebrew Bible reflects are there as types, impressions from the full, prior reality that is Christ.

The difficulties experienced in the contemporary Church, since the Enlightenment, have largely stemmed from the anxiety that a historical, critical reading seems to contradict a typological reading. The result is that some calls have been heard to remodel the faith, and some to cancel the claims of historical reason. Whatever the merits of such new orthodoxies, they cannot claim the support of the New Testament. Here, no text is sufficient by itself to deliver the truth, whether by means of ancient or modern methods of reading. Rather, the enduring reality of the kingdom as preached by Jesus and vindicated by his resurrection is the light by virtue of which the Hebrew Bible shines as a lamp in a dark place. Without a vision of the kingdom, there is no faith in Jesus, and apart from that, Christian interpretation simply does not exist.

Index